**The Driving School**

 KU-169-169

HALF PRICE DRIVING LESSON

Save £24 when you pre-pay for a further 12 lessons

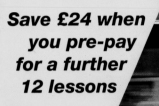

To book your lesson call free on

0800 60 70 80

Quote: AA Book Offer

HALF PRICE LESSON MUST BE TAKEN BY 31.12. 2000

Some of the benefits of learning to drive with the AA :

- Personal tuition from fully qualified instructors

- Top-of-the-range dual-controlled Ford Fiesta 1.25 Ghia with air conditioning and power steering

- Offers and discounts in your Congratulations Pack when you pass including a free hour of motorway tuition

Learning to drive with the AA costs less than you think

AA The Driving School

HALF PRICE DRIVING LESSON

TERMS AND CONDITIONS

1. **The half price lesson must be taken by 31 December 2000.**
2. The offer is not open to existing pupils of AA The Driving School.
3. This voucher cannot be used in conjunction with any other offer.
4. The lesson will be booked subject to availability.
5. Only one voucher per person.
6. Offer applies to lessons taken in the UK mainland only.
7. The offer is not open to employees of the AA Group or their families
8. This offer is valid for lessons booked with AA The Driving School through the freephone booking service only.
9. Original vouchers only – no photocopies.
10. No cash equivalent available.
11. The offer is only open to holders of a provisional driving licence for private motor car tuition at the time of taking the lesson.

The Promoter: Automobile Association Developments Limited, trading as AA The Driving School, Norfolk House, Priestley Road,Basingstoke, Hampshire, RG24 9NY.

www.theaa.co.uk

TO THE CUSTOMER

Once you have booked your lesson, hand this voucher plus the remaining half of the cost of the lesson (confirmed at the time of booking) to the instructor.

TO THE INSTRUCTOR

Please complete the details below and attach this 50% discount voucher to your weekly worksheet in order to qualify for payment of the outstanding balance.

PUPIL'S NAME

PUPIL'S NUMBER

INSTRUCTOR'S NAME

INSTRUCTOR'S NUMBER

AA DRIVING TEST THEORY

THE OFFICIAL
QUESTIONS & ANSWERS

AA Publishing

Produced by AA Publishing.

© The Automobile Association 1999
First edition 1996
Reprinted 1996 (5 times)
Second edition with revised questions 1997
Reprinted 1998 (twice)
Third edition with revised questions 1998
Reprinted with amendments 1998 (twice)
Fourth edition with revised questions 1999

Crown copyright material reproduced under licence from the
Controller of HMSO and the Driving Standards Agency.

ISBN 0 7495 2064 7

All rights reserved. No part of this publication may be
reproduced, stored in a retrieval system, or transmitted in
any form or by any means – electronic, photocopying,
recording or otherwise – unless the written permission of
the publisher has been obtained beforehand.

Published by AA Publishing (a trading name of Automobile
Association Developments Limited, whose registered office
is Norfolk House, Priestley Road, Basingstoke, Hampshire
RG24 9NY; registered number 1878835).

The AA's Web site address is www.theaa.co.uk

The contents of this book are believed correct at the time of
printing. Nevertheless, the publishers cannot be held
responsible for any errors or omissions or for changes in the
details given in this book or for the consequences of any
reliance on the information provided by the same.

Colour separation by Anton Graphics, Andover.
Printed by George Over Limited, London and Rugby.
Editor: Jane Gregory.

THE THEORY TEST

Since July 1996 learner drivers must pass a theory test
and a practical test to get a full driving licence.

YOUR QUESTIONS ANSWERED

Q. *Why a theory test?*

A. To check that drivers know and understand what
to do before they do it.

Q. *How does it work?*

A. The test consists of 35 multiple-choice questions.

Q. *What is a multiple-choice question?*

A. One with 4, 5 or 6 answers to choose from.

Q. *What does the test cover?*

A. All the topics listed in this book.

ABOUT THIS BOOK

This book will help you to pass your theory test:

* the preface provides useful advice and information

* the questions and answers are arranged under the
  14 official syllabus topics

* questions dealing with related aspects of a topic
  are grouped together

* all the correct answers are at the back of the book.

> Questions marked with an **NI** symbol are those that will not be found
> in Theory Test papers in Northern Ireland.

While every effort has been made to include the widest possible range of questions available at the time
of printing, the Government may from time to time change, add or remove questions, and the publisher
cannot be held responsible for questions that may appear on a question paper which were not available
for inclusion in this book.

HOW TO USE THIS BOOK

1. Look at the list of topics on this page and turn to one you find interesting.
2. Read the first question and tick your choice of answer(s).
3. Check your answer(s) against the correct answers at the back of the book.
4. Make sure you understand the answers before you try the next question.

WARNING

Do **not** try too many questions at once.

Do **not** try to learn the answers by heart.

The order of the answers in this book may be different from how they are arranged in the actual test – so do **not** try to memorise the order.

HOW TO ANSWER THE QUESTIONS

Each question has four, five or six answers. You must mark the boxes with the correct answer or answers. Each question tells you how many answers to mark.

Study each question carefully, making sure you understand. Look carefully at any diagram, drawing or photograph. Before you look at the answers given, decide what you think the right answer may be. You can then select the answer that matches the one you had decided on. If you follow this system, you will avoid being confused by answers which appear to be similar.

You now have to pass two driving tests before you can apply for a full driving licence. The new test, introduced in July 1996, is a written theory test, and this book contains the **official questions** that you may have to answer. You will have to pass your theory test before you can apply for the practical test.

PREPARING FOR BOTH TESTS

You are strongly recommended to prepare for the theory test at the **same time** as you develop your skills behind the wheel. Obviously, there are many similarities between the two tests – it is all about helping to make you a safer driver on today's busy roads. By preparing for both tests at the same time, you will reinforce your knowledge and understanding of all aspects of driving and you will improve your chances of passing both tests first time.

THE THEORY TEST

You will have 40 minutes to complete the paper and all questions are multiple-choice. The Government may change the pass mark from time to time. Your driving school will be able to tell you if there has been a change. Also, the Government may, from time to time, introduce new or amended questions. However, if you are fully prepared on each topic, you will be in a position to answer any question.

SELECTING A DRIVING SCHOOL

When you select a driving school to teach you the practical skills, make sure they are prepared to advise and help you with the theory test. Good driving schools will provide theory practice papers for you to complete before you take the real test. These papers will help you judge your level of knowledge and help with your preparation. Check with friends who have been taught recently, and make sure you understand the difference between an instructor who displays a pink badge (a trainee instructor) and one who displays a green badge (a fully qualified instructor). Price is important, so find out whether the school offers any discounts for blocks or courses of lessons paid in advance; if you decide to pay in advance, make sure the driving school is reputable. If lesson prices are very low, ask yourself 'why?' And don't forget to ask about the car you'll be learning to drive in. Is it modern and reliable? Is it insured?

WHAT TO EXPECT

As with all courses, there are a number of subjects you will need to master. All good driving schools will have available a progress sheet and syllabus which sets out all the skills you will need and keeps a record of your progress. You will probably find that if you take a two-hour lesson every week, your rate of progress will surprise you!

It is important to book and take your theory test at an early stage in your course of practical lessons.

After a few hours of tuition the instructor will discuss with you a structured course to suit your needs and you can agree on the likely date when you will be ready to take the practical test. You can then apply for a practical test appointment; this will give you added incentive to prepare thoroughly.

THE AA'S DRIVING SCHOOL

The AA has a driving school staffed by fully qualified instructors, who are all familiar with this book, the theory test and the practical test. Why not give them a try? You can ring for details on freephone 0800 60 70 80.

KNOWLEDGE, SKILLS AND ATTITUDE

Being a good driver is more than just having the knowledge and the skills – it is about applying them with the right attitude. No one is a 'natural' or a 'perfect driver'. All drivers make mistakes. Being careful, courteous and considerate to other road users will complement the skills and knowledge you will acquire in the coming weeks and make you a good driver.

Preface by **Linda Hatswell** and **Nick Bravery** – AA The Driving School

навыкиэть

1 When turning your car in the road you should always

Mark one answer
- [ ] **A.** Overhang the kerb *край тротуара (обочина)*
- [ ] **B.** Use a driveway
- [x] **C.** Check all around for other road users ✓
- [ ] **D.** Keep your hand on the handbrake

2 Before you make a U-turn in the road, you should

Mark one answer
- [ ] **A.** give an arm signal as well as using your indicators
- [ ] **B.** signal so that other drivers can slow down for you
- [x] **C.** look over your shoulder for a final check ✓
- [ ] **D.** select a higher gear than normal

3 As a driver what does the term 'Blind Spot' mean?

Mark one answer
- [ ] **A.** An area covered by your right-hand mirror
- [ ] **B.** An area not covered by your headlamps
- [ ] **C.** An area covered by your left-hand mirror
- [x] **D.** An area not seen in your mirrors ✓

4 Objects hanging from your interior mirror may

Mark two answers
- [x] **A.** Restrict your view ✓ *ограничивать*
- [ ] **B.** Improve your driving
- [x] **C.** Distract your attention ✓ *отвлекать*
- [ ] **D.** Help your concentration

5 You are most likely to lose concentration when driving if you

Mark two answers
- [x] **A.** use a mobile phone ✓
- [x] **B.** listen to very loud music ✓
- [ ] **C.** switch on the heated rear window
- [ ] **D.** look at the door mirrors

6 Which FOUR are most likely to cause you to lose concentration while you are driving?

Mark four answers
- [x] **A.** Using a mobile phone ✓
- [x] **B.** Talking into a microphone
- [x] **C.** Tuning your car radio ✓
- [x] **D.** Looking at a map ✓
- [ ] **E.** Checking the mirrors
- [ ] **F.** Using the demisters

7 What, according to *The Driving Manual*, do the letters MSM mean?

Mark one answer
- [x] **A.** Mirror, signal, manoeuvre ✓
- [ ] **B.** Manoeuvre, signal, mirror
- [ ] **C.** Mirror, speed, manoeuvre
- [ ] **D.** Manoeuvre, speed, mirror

8 You are driving on a wet road. You have to stop your vehicle in an emergency. You should

Mark one answer
- [ ] **A.** Apply the handbrake and footbrake together ✓
- [x] **B.** Keep both hands on the wheel
- [ ] **C.** Select reverse gear
- [ ] **D.** Give an arm signal

9 As you approach this bridge you should

Mark three answers

- [ ] **A.** Move into the middle of the road to get a better view
- [x] **B.** Slow down ✓
- [ ] **C.** Get over the bridge as quickly as possible
- [x] **D.** Consider using your horn ✓
- [ ] **E.** Find another route *nych; uangabaeno*
- [x] **F.** Beware of pedestrians
  onecasace

10 When following a large vehicle you should keep well back because

Mark one answer

- [ ] **A.** It allows you to corner more quickly
- [ ] **B.** It helps the large vehicle to stop more easily
- [x] **C.** It allows the driver to see you in the mirrors ✓
- [ ] **D.** It helps you keep out of the wind

11 In which of these situations should you avoid overtaking?
onouen

Mark one answer

- [ ] **A.** Just after a bend
- [ ] **B.** In a one-way street
- [ ] **C.** On a 30mph road ✓
- [x] **D.** Approaching a dip in the road

12 Which of the following may cause loss of concentration on a long journey?

Mark four answers

- [x] **A.** Loud music
- [x] **B.** Arguing with a passenger ✓
- [x] **C.** Using a mobile phone ✓
- [x] **D.** Putting in a cassette tape
- [ ] **E.** Stopping regularly to rest
- [ ] **F.** Pulling up to tune the radio

13 You should not use a mobile phone whilst driving

Mark one answer

- [ ] **A.** Until you are satisfied that no other traffic is near
- [ ] **B.** Unless you are able to drive one handed
- [x] **C.** Because it might distract your attention from the road ahead ✓
- [ ] **D.** Because reception is poor when the engine is running

14 Your vehicle is fitted with a hands-free phone system. Using this equipment whilst driving
ocuaufu

Mark one answer

- [ ] **A.** Is quite safe as long as you slow down
- [x] **B.** Could distract your attention from the road
- [ ] **C.** Is recommended by the Highway Code ?
- [ ] **D.** Could be very good for road safety

15 Using a hands-free phone is likely to

Mark one answer
- A. Improve your safety ✓
- B. Increase your concentration
- C. Reduce your view
- ☑ D. Divert your attention

16 Using a mobile phone while you are driving

Mark one answer
- A. Is acceptable in a vehicle with power steering *рулить*
- B. Will reduce your field of vision
- ☑ C. Could distract your attention from the road ✓
- D. Will affect your vehicle's electronic systems

17 *стрелка* The white arrow means that you should not plan to

Mark one answer
- A. Slow down
- B. Turn right
- ☑ C. Overtake ✓
- D. Turn left

18 This road marking warns

Mark one answer
- A. Drivers to use the hard shoulder
- B. Overtaking drivers there is a bend to the left
- ☑ C. Overtaking drivers to move back to the left ✓
- D. Drivers that it is safe to overtake

19 You are driving along this narrow country road. When passing the cyclist you should drive

Mark one answer
- A. Slowly sounding the horn as you pass
- B. Quickly leaving plenty of room
- ☑ C. Slowly leaving plenty of room ✓
- D. Quickly sounding the horn as you pass

20 You are driving a vehicle fitted with a hand-held telephone. To use the telephone you should

Mark one answer

- [ ] **A.** Reduce your speed ✗
- [✓] **B.** Find a safe place to stop ✓
- [ ] **C.** Steer the vehicle with one hand
- [ ] **D.** Be particularly careful at junctions

21 Your mobile phone rings while you are driving on the motorway. Before answering you should

Mark one answer

- [ ] **A.** Reduce your speed to 50mph
- [ ] **B.** Pull up on the hard shoulder
- [ ] **C.** Move into the left-hand lane
- [✓] **D.** Stop in a safe place ✓

22 To answer a call on your mobile phone when driving, you should

Mark one answer

- [ ] **A.** Reduce your speed wherever you are
- [✓] **B.** Stop in a proper and convenient place
- [ ] **C.** Keep the call time to a minimum ✓
- [ ] **D.** Slow down and allow others to overtake

23 You want to use a mobile phone whilst driving. You should only use the phone

Mark one answer

- [✓] **A.** After stopping in a suitable place ✓
- [ ] **B.** When driving on quiet, minor roads
- [ ] **C.** If you are driving on a motorway
- [ ] **D.** If you feel your driving will be unaffected

24 Your mobile phone rings while you are travelling. You should

Mark one answer

- [ ] **A.** Stop immediately
- [ ] **B.** Answer it immediately
- [✓] **C.** Pull up in a suitable place ✓
- [ ] **D.** Pull up at the nearest kerb ?

25 You should ONLY use a mobile phone when

Mark one answer

- [ ] **A.** Receiving a call
- [✓] **B.** Suitably parked ✓
- [ ] **C.** Driving at less than 30mph
- [ ] **D.** Driving an automatic vehicle

26 What is the safest way to use a mobile phone in your vehicle?

Mark one answer

- [ ] **A.** Use hands-free equipment
- [✓] **B.** Find a suitable place to stop ✓
- [ ] **C.** Drive slowly on a quiet road
- [ ] **D.** Direct your call through the operator

27 Why should you be parked safely before using a mobile phone?

Mark one answer

- [ ] **A.** Because reception is better when stopped
- [✓] **B.** So control of your vehicle is not affected
- [ ] **C.** So a proper conversation can be held ✓
- [ ] **D.** Because the car electrics will be affected

28 On a long motorway journey boredom can cause you to feel sleepy. You should

Mark two answers

- ☑ **A.** Leave the motorway and find a safe place to stop ✓
- ☐ **B.** Keep looking around at the surrounding landscape *все окружающие вещи*
- ☐ **C.** Drive faster to complete your journey sooner
- ☑ **D.** Ensure a supply of fresh air into your vehicle ✓
- ☐ **E.** Increase the volume of the car sound system
- ☐ **F.** Stop on the hard shoulder for a rest

29 You are driving at night and are *ослеплен* dazzled by the headlights of an oncoming car. You should

Mark one answer

- ☑ **A.** Slow down or stop
- ☐ **B.** Close your eyes
- ☐ **C.** Flash your headlights +
- ☐ **D.** Pull down the sun visor ✓

30 *раньше* You are driving at dusk. You should switch your lights on

Mark two answers

- ☑ **A.** Even when street lights are not lit
- ☑ **B.** So others can see you ✓
- ☐ **C.** Only when others have done so
- ☐ **D.** Only when street lights are lit

31 Why are these yellow lines painted across the road?

Mark one answer

- ☐ **A.** To help you choose the correct lane
- ☐ **B.** To help you keep the correct separation distance ✓
- ☑ **C.** To make you aware of your speed
- ☐ **D.** To tell you the distance to the roundabout

32 To overtake safely, which of the following applies?

Mark one answer

- ☑ **A.** Check the speed and position of following traffic ✓
- ☐ **B.** Cut back in sharply when you have passed the vehicle
- ☐ **C.** Get in close behind before signalling to move out
- ☐ **D.** Steer round the vehicle sharply *неверно*

33 A pelican crossing that crosses the road in a STRAIGHT line and has a central island MUST be treated as

Mark one answer

- A. One crossing in daylight only
- ✓ B. One complete crossing *когда в одну линию;*
- C. Two separate crossings ✓
- D. Two crossings during darkness

а если не в линию - два разных перехода

34 At a pelican crossing the flashing amber light means you should

Mark one answer

- A. Stop and wait for the green light
- B. Stop and wait for the red light
- C. Give way to pedestrians waiting to cross
- ✓ D. Give way to pedestrians already on the crossing ✓

35 You are approaching a pelican crossing. The amber light is flashing. You must

Mark one answer

- ✓ A. Give way to pedestrians who are crossing *база*
- B. Encourage pedestrians to cross
- C. Not move until the green light appears
- D. Stop even if the crossing is clear ✓

36 You are driving towards a zebra crossing. Pedestrians are waiting to cross. You should

Mark one answer

- A. Give way to the elderly and infirm only
- ✓ B. Slow down and prepare to stop ✓
- C. Use your headlamps to indicate they can cross
- D. Wave at them to cross the road

37 You have stopped at a pedestrian crossing, to allow pedestrians to cross. You should

Mark one answer

- ✓ A. Wait until they have crossed
- B. Edge your vehicle forward slowly
- C. Wait, revving your engine ✓ *ха-ха !*
- D. Signal to pedestrians to cross *дурацкий смысл*

38 *погрошес* You should never wave people across at pedestrian crossings because

Mark one answer

- ✓ A. There may be another vehicle coming
- B. They may not be looking ✓
- C. It is safer for you to carry on
- D. They may not be ready to cross

39 Why should you give an arm signal on approach to a zebra crossing?

Mark three answers

- ✓ A. To warn following traffic
- B. To let pedestrians know you are not stopping
- ✓ C. To let pedestrians know you are slowing down
- ✓ D. To warn oncoming traffic
- E. To warn traffic you intend to turn

40 At zebra crossings you should

Mark one answer

- A. Rev your engine to encourage pedestrians to cross quickly
- B. Park only on the zigzag lines on the left
- ✓ C. Always leave it clear in traffic queues
- D. Wave pedestrians to cross if you intend to wait for them

41 You stop for pedestrians waiting to cross at a zebra crossing. They do not start to cross. What should you do?

Mark one answer
- ✓ **A.** Be patient and wait
- **B.** Sound your horn
- **C.** Drive on
- **D.** Wave them to cross ✓ *терпение!*

42 At puffin crossings which light will not show to a driver?

Mark one answer
- ✓ **A.** Flashing amber
- **B.** Red
- **C.** Steady amber
- **D.** Green

43 You are approaching a red light at a puffin crossing. Pedestrians are on the crossing. The red light will stay on until

Mark one answer
- **A.** You start to edge forward on to the crossing
- ✓ **B.** The pedestrians have reached a safe position
- **C.** The pedestrians are clear of the front of your vehicle
- **D.** A driver from the opposite direction reaches the crossing

44 At a puffin crossing what colour follows the green signal?

Mark one answer
- **A.** Steady red ✓
- **B.** Flashing amber —
- ✓ **C.** Steady amber —
- **D.** Flashing green

45 You could use the 'Two-Second Rule'

Mark one answer
- **A.** Before restarting the engine after it has stalled
- ✓ **B.** To keep a safe gap from the vehicle in front ✓
- **C.** Before using the 'mirror, signal, manoeuvre' routine
- **D.** When emerging on wet roads

46 A two-second gap between yourself and the car in front is sufficient when conditions are *достаточно*

Mark one answer
- **A.** Wet ✓
- ✓ **B.** Good
- **C.** Damp
- **D.** Foggy

47 In fast traffic a two-second gap may be enough only when conditions are

Mark one answer
- ✓ **A.** Dry ✓
- **B.** Wet
- **C.** Damp
- **D.** Foggy

48 'Tailgating' means

Mark one answer

- ☐ **A.** Using the rear door of a hatchback car
- ☐ **B.** Reversing into a parking space
- ☑ **C.** Following another vehicle too closely ✓
- ☐ **D.** Driving with rear fog lights on

Mark one answer

- ☑ **A.** Give you a good view of the road ahead ✓
- ☐ **B.** Stop following traffic from rushing through the junction
- ☐ **C.** Prevent traffic behind you from overtaking
- ☐ **D.** Allow you to hurry through the traffic lights if they change

49 You are driving on a clear night. There is a steady stream of oncoming traffic. The national speed limit applies. Which lights should you use?

Mark one answer

- ☐ **A.** Full beam headlights
- ☐ **B.** Sidelights
- ☑ **C.** Dipped headlights ✓
- ☐ **D.** Fog lights

52 You are driving behind a large goods vehicle. It signals left but steers to the right. You should

Mark one answer

- ☑ **A.** Slow down and let the vehicle turn ✓
- ☐ **B.** Drive on, keeping to the left
- ☐ **C.** Overtake on the right of it
- ☐ **D.** Hold your speed and sound your horn

50 Following this vehicle too closely is unwise because

Mark one answer

- ☐ **A.** Your brakes will overheat
- ☐ **B.** Your view ahead is increased
- ☐ **C.** Your engine will overheat
- ☑ **D.** Your view ahead is reduced

53 You are following a vehicle on a wet road. You should leave a time gap of at least

Mark one answer

- ☐ **A.** One second
- ☐ **B.** Two seconds
- ☐ **C.** Three seconds
- ☑ **D.** Four seconds ✓

51 You are following this lorry. You should keep well back from it to

54 You are driving along this road. The red van cuts in close in front of you. What should you do?

Mark one answer
- [ ] **A.** Accelerate to get closer to the red van
- [ ] **B.** Give a long blast on the horn
- [x] **C.** Drop back to leave the correct separation distance √
- [ ] **D.** Flash your headlights several times —

в заключение и для успокоения совесн

55 You are in a line of traffic. The driver behind you is following very closely. What action should you take?

НЕПОНЯТНО !!! !!!

Mark one answer
- [ ] **A.** Ignore the following driver and continue to drive within the speed limit ?
- [x] **B.** Slow down, gradually increasing the gap between you and the vehicle in front
- [ ] **C.** Signal left and wave the following driver past √
- [ ] **D.** Move over to a position just left of the centre line of the road

Редко притормозить и пусть он первый едет !...

56 You are driving at the legal speed limit. A vehicle comes up quickly behind, flashing its headlamps. You should

Mark one answer
- [ ] **A.** Accelerate to make a gap behind you
- [ ] **B.** Touch the brakes to show your brake lights Ха-ха! Так и и сделаю...
- [ ] **C.** Maintain your speed and prevent the vehicle from overtaking
- [x] **D.** Allow the vehicle to overtake √
его ответственность

57 You are waiting in a traffic queue at night. To avoid dazzling following drivers you should

// Когда в пробке - только на ручной тормоз ...

Mark one answer
- [x] **A.** Apply the handbrake only
- [ ] **B.** Apply the footbrake only
- [ ] **C.** Switch off your headlights
- [ ] **D.** Use both the handbrake and footbrake

превысил
58 When are you allowed to exceed the maximum speed limit?
Mark one answer
- [ ] **A.** Between midnight and 6am
- [x] **B.** At no time √
- [ ] **C.** When overtaking
- [ ] **D.** When the road is clear

Никогда не превышаа лимит скорости.

59 You are driving at the legal speed limit. A vehicle behind wants to overtake. Should you try to prevent the driver overtaking?
Mark one answer
- [ ] **A.** No, unless it is safe to do so
- [ ] **B.** Yes, because the other driver is acting dangerously
- [x] **C.** No, not at any time √
- [ ] **D.** Yes, because the other driver is breaking the law

Все под его ответственность!

60 You are driving in traffic at the speed limit for the road. The driver behind is trying to overtake. You should
Mark one answer
- [ ] **A.** Move closer to the car ahead, so the driver behind has no room to overtake
- [ ] **B.** Wave the driver behind to overtake when it is safe √
- [x] **C.** Keep a steady course and allow the driver behind to overtake ━
- [ ] **D.** Accelerate to get away from the driver behind

здравый смысл

61 You are driving at night on an unlit road following a slower moving vehicle. You should

неосвещен (handwritten)

Mark one answer
- [ ] **A.** Flash your headlights
- [x] **B.** Use dipped beam headlights
- [ ] **C.** Switch off your headlights
- [ ] **D.** Use full beam headlights

нельзя слепить (handwritten)

62 A long, heavily-laden lorry is taking a long time to overtake you. What should you do?

Mark one answer
- [ ] **A.** Speed up
- [x] **B.** Slow down ✓ *nice to be nice*
- [ ] **C.** Hold your speed
- [ ] **D.** Change direction !

Вежливость прежде всего! (handwritten)

63 You are driving a slow-moving vehicle on a narrow winding road. You should

Mark one answer
- [ ] **A.** Keep well out to stop vehicles overtaking dangerously
- [ ] **B.** Wave following vehicles past you if you think they can overtake quickly
- [x] **C.** Pull in safely when you can, to let following vehicles overtake
- [ ] **D.** Give a left signal when it is safe for vehicles to overtake you ✓

64 You are driving a slow-moving vehicle on a narrow road. When traffic wishes to overtake you should

Mark one answer
- [ ] **A.** Take no action ✓
- [ ] **B.** Put your hazard warning lights on
- [ ] **C.** Stop immediately and wave it on
- [x] **D.** Pull in safely as soon as you can do so ✓

отпугивать! (handwritten)

65 You are driving a slow-moving vehicle on a narrow winding road. In order to let other vehicles overtake you should

Mark one answer
- [ ] **A.** Wave to them to pass
- [x] **B.** Pull in when you can ✓
- [ ] **C.** Show a left turn signal ✓
- [ ] **D.** Keep left and hold your speed

66 Which of the following vehicles will use blue flashing beacons?

Mark three answers
- [ ] **A.** Motorway maintenance
- [ ] **B.** Bomb disposal ✓
- [ ] **C.** Blood transfusion ✓
- [ ] **D.** Police patrol ✓
- [ ] **E.** Breakdown recovery

Голубые лампы - полиция, саперы, кровь (handwritten)

67 Which THREE of these emergency services might have blue flashing beacons?

Mark three answers
- [ ] **A.** Coastguard ✓
- [ ] **B.** Bomb disposal ✓
- [ ] **C.** Gritting lorries
- [ ] **D.** Animal ambulances
- [ ] **E.** Mountain rescue ✓
- [ ] **F.** Doctors' cars

Кто какого цвета - голубой, зеленый, оранж (handwritten)

68 When being followed by an ambulance showing a flashing blue beacon you should

Mark one answer
- [x] **A.** Pull over as soon as safely possible to let it pass ✓
- [ ] **B.** Accelerate hard to get away from it
- [ ] **C.** Maintain your speed and course
- [ ] **D.** Brake harshly and immediately stop in the road

69 You see a car showing a flashing green beacon. Should you give way to it?

Mark one answer
- [x] **A.** Yes, it is a doctor going to an emergency
- [ ] **B.** Yes, it is a fire crew support vehicle
- [ ] **C.** No, it is a slow-moving vehicle
- [ ] **D.** No, it is a breakdown vehicle

70 What type of emergency vehicle is fitted with a green flashing beacon?

Mark one answer
- [ ] **A.** Fire engine
- [ ] **B.** Road gritter
- [ ] **C.** Ambulance
- [x] **D.** Doctor's car ✓

71 A flashing green beacon on a vehicle means

Mark one answer
- [ ] **A.** Police on non-urgent duties
- [x] **B.** Doctor on an emergency call ✓
- [ ] **C.** Road safety patrol operating
- [ ] **D.** Gritting in progress

72 A vehicle has a flashing green beacon. What does this mean?

Mark one answer
- [x] **A.** A doctor is answering an emergency call ✓
- [ ] **B.** The vehicle is slow-moving
- [ ] **C.** It is a motorway police patrol vehicle
- [ ] **D.** A vehicle is carrying hazardous chemicals

73 Diamond-shaped signs give instructions to

Mark one answer
- [x] **A.** Tram drivers ✓
- [ ] **B.** Bus drivers
- [ ] **C.** Lorry drivers
- [ ] **D.** Taxi drivers

74 On a road where trams operate, which of these vehicles will be most at risk from the tram rails?

Mark one answer
- [ ] **A.** Cars ✓
- [x] **B.** Cycles
- [ ] **C.** Buses
- [ ] **D.** Lorries

75 At unmarked junctions where tram lines cross over roads, who has priority?

Mark one answer
- [ ] **A.** Cars
- [ ] **B.** Motorcycles
- [✓] **C.** Trams ✓
- [ ] **D.** Buses

76 A bus is stopped at a bus stop ahead of you. Its right-hand indicator is flashing. You should

Mark one answer
- [ ] **A.** Flash your headlights and slow down
- [✓] **B.** Slow down and give way if it is safe to do so ✓
- [ ] **C.** Sound your horn and keep going
- [ ] **D.** Slow down and then sound your horn

77 A bus lane on your left shows no times of operation. This means it is

Mark one answer
- [ ] **A.** Not in operation at all
- [ ] **B.** Only in operation at peak times
- [✓] **C.** In operation 24 hours a day ✓
- [ ] **D.** Only in operation in daylight hours

78 You should ONLY flash your headlights to other road users

Mark one answer
- [ ] **A.** To show that you are giving way
- [ ] **B.** To show that you are about to reverse
- [ ] **C.** To tell them that you have right of way
- [✓] **D.** To let them know that you are there ✓

79 What should you use your horn for?

Mark one answer
- [✓] **A.** To alert others to your presence ✓
- [ ] **B.** To allow you right of way
- [ ] **C.** To greet other road users
- [ ] **D.** To signal your annoyance

80 A vehicle pulls out in front of you at a junction. What should you do?

Mark one answer
- [ ] **A.** Swerve past it and blow your horn
- [ ] **B.** Flash your headlights and drive up close behind
- [✓] **C.** Slow down and be ready to stop ✓
- [ ] **D.** Accelerate past it immediately

81 You are in a one-way street and want to turn right. You should position yourself

Mark one answer
- ☑ **A.** In the right-hand lane ✓
- ☐ **B.** In the left-hand lane
- ☐ **C.** In either lane, depending on the traffic
- ☐ **D.** Just left of the centre line

82 You wish to turn right ahead. Why should you take up the correct position in good time?

Mark one answer
- ☐ **A.** To allow other drivers to pull out in front of you
- ☐ **B.** To give a better view into the road that you're joining
- ☑ **C.** To help other road users know what you intend to do ✓
- ☐ **D.** To allow drivers to pass you on the right

83 You are driving along a country road. A horse and rider are approaching. What should you do?

Mark two answers
- ☐ **A.** Increase your speed
- ☐ **B.** Sound your horn
- ☐ **C.** Flash your headlights
- ☑ **D.** Drive slowly past ✓
- ☑ **E.** Give plenty of room ✓
- ☐ **F.** Rev your engine

84 A person herding sheep asks you to stop. You should

Mark one answer
- ☐ **A.** Ignore them as they have no authority
- ☑ **B.** Stop and switch off your engine
- ☐ **C.** Continue on but drive slowly ✓
- ☐ **D.** Try and get past quickly

85 When overtaking a horse and rider you should

Mark one answer
- ☐ **A.** sound your horn as a warning
- ☐ **B.** go past as quickly as possible
- ☐ **C.** flash your headlights as a warning
- ☑ **D.** go past slowly and carefully ✓

86 Which of the following are at greatest risk from other road users?

Mark one answer
- ☑ **A.** Motorcyclists
- ☐ **B.** Lorry drivers
- ☐ **C.** Learner car drivers ✓
- ☐ **D.** Busy bus drivers

87 When should you especially check the engine oil level?

Mark one answer
- [x] **A.** Before a long journey
- [ ] **B.** When the engine is hot
- [ ] **C.** Early in the morning
- [ ] **D.** Every 6,000 miles ✓

88 Which of these, if allowed to get low, could cause an accident?

Mark one answer
- [ ] **A.** Antifreeze level
- [x] **B.** Brake fluid level ✓
- [ ] **C.** Battery water level
- [ ] **D.** Radiator coolant level

89 Which FOUR of these **must** be in good working order for your car to be roadworthy?

Mark four answers
- [ ] **A.** Temperature gauge
- [x] **B.** Speedometer ✓
- [x] **C.** Windscreen washers ✓
- [x] **D.** Windscreen wipers ✓
- [ ] **E.** Oil warning light
- [x] **F.** Horn

90 Which THREE does the law require you to keep in good condition?

Mark three answers
- [ ] **A.** Gears
- [ ] **B.** Transmission
- [x] **C.** Headlights
- [x] **D.** Windscreen
- [x] **E.** Seat belts

91 New petrol-engined cars must be fitted with catalytic converters. The reason for this is to

Mark one answer
- [ ] **A.** Control exhaust noise levels
- [ ] **B.** Prolong the life of the exhaust system
- [ ] **C.** Allow the exhaust system to be recycled
- [x] **D.** Reduce harmful exhaust emissions ✓

92 Which TWO are badly affected if the tyres are under-inflated?

Mark two answers
- [x] **A.** Braking
- [x] **B.** Steering
- [ ] **C.** Changing gear
- [ ] **D.** Parking

93 What can cause heavy steering?

Mark one answer
- [ ] **A.** Driving on ice
- [ ] **B.** Badly worn brakes
- [ ] **C.** Over-inflated tyres
- [x] **D.** Under-inflated tyres

94 Your car is fitted with power-assisted steering. This will make the steering seem

Mark one answer
- [x] **A.** Lighter ✓
- [ ] **B.** Heavier
- [ ] **C.** Quieter
- [ ] **D.** Noisier

95 It is essential that tyre pressures are checked regularly. When should this be done?

Mark one answer
- [ ] **A.** After any lengthy journey
- [ ] **B.** After driving at high speed
- [ ] **C.** When tyres are hot
- [x] **D.** When tyres are cold

96 It is important that tyre pressures are correct. They should be checked at least

Mark one answer
- [ ] **A.** Every time the vehicle is serviced
- [x] **B.** Once a week
- [ ] **C.** Once a month
- [ ] **D.** Every time the vehicle has an MOT test ✓

97 Driving with under-inflated tyres can affect

Mark two answers
- [ ] **A.** Engine temperature
- [x] **B.** Fuel consumption
- [x] **C.** Braking ✓
- [ ] **D.** Oil pressure

98 A police officer orders you to stop. He finds you have a faulty tyre. Who is responsible for the tyre?

Mark one answer
- [ ] **A.** The previous owner
- [ ] **B.** Whoever services the car
- [x] **C.** You, the driver ✓
- [ ] **D.** Whoever issued the MOT certificate

99 It is illegal to drive with tyres that

Mark one answer
- [ ] **A.** Have been bought second-hand
- [x] **B.** Have a large deep cut in the side wall
- [ ] **C.** Are of different makes
- [ ] **D.** Are of different tread patterns

100 The legal minimum depth of tread for car tyres over three-quarters of the breadth is

Mark one answer
- [ ] **A.** 1mm
- [x] **B.** 1.6mm
- [ ] **C.** 2.5mm ✓
- [ ] **D.** 4mm

101 Excessive or uneven tyre wear can be caused by faults in the

Mark two answers
- [ ] **A.** Gearbox
- [x] **B.** Braking system
- [x] **C.** Suspension
- [ ] **D.** Exhaust system

102 There is vibration on your steering wheel as you drive. You should check that the

Mark one answer
- [ ] **A.** Doors are closed
- [x] **B.** Wheels are balanced ✓
- [ ] **C.** Exhaust is not loose
- [ ] **D.** Engine oil level is correct

103 Your vehicle pulls to one side when braking. You should

Mark one answer
- ☐ **A.** Change the tyres around
- ☑ **B.** Consult your garage as soon as possible ✓
- ☐ **C.** Pump the pedal when braking
- ☐ **D.** Use your handbrake at the same time

104 The main cause of brake fade is *bunyob*

Mark one answer
- ☑ **A.** The brakes overheating
- ☐ **B.** Air in the brake fluid ✓
- ☐ **C.** Oil on the brakes
- ☐ **D.** The brakes out of adjustment

105 Your anti-lock brakes warning light stays on. You should

Mark one answer
- ☐ **A.** Check the brake fluid level
- ☐ **B.** Check the footbrake freeplay
- ☐ **C.** Check that the handbrake is released
- ☑ **D.** Have the brakes checked immediately ✓

106 If you notice a strong smell of petrol as you drive along you should

Mark one answer
- ☐ **A.** Not worry, as it is only exhaust fumes
- ☐ **B.** Carry on at a reduced speed
- ☐ **C.** Expect it to stop in a few miles
- ☑ **D.** Stop and investigate the problem ✓

107 What does this instrument panel light mean when lit?

Mark one answer
- ☐ **A.** Gear lever in park ✓
- ☐ **B.** Gear lever in neutral
- ☑ **C.** Handbrake on
- ☐ **D.** Handbrake off

108 When must you use dipped headlights during the day?

Mark one answer
- ☐ **A.** All the time
- ☐ **B.** Along narrow streets
- ☑ **C.** In poor visibility ✓
- ☐ **D.** When parking

109 Which instrument panel warning light would show that headlamps are on full beam?

Mark one answer
- ☑ **A.** ✓
- ☐ **B.**
- ☐ **C.**
- ☐ **D.**

110 While driving, this warning light on your dashboard comes on. It means

Mark one answer
- ☑ **A.** A fault in the braking system
- ☐ **B.** The engine oil is low
- ☐ **C.** A rear light has failed
- ☐ **D.** Your seat belt is not fastened

111 You are driving on a motorway. The traffic ahead is braking sharply because of an accident. How could you warn following traffic?

Mark one answer
- ☑ **A.** Briefly use the hazard warning lights
- ☐ **B.** Switch on the hazard warning lights continuously
- ☐ **C.** Briefly use the rear fog lights
- ☐ **D.** Switch on the headlamps continuously

112 When may you use hazard warning lights?

Mark one answer
- ☐ **A.** To park alongside another car
- ☐ **B.** To park on double yellow lines
- ☐ **C.** When you are being towed
- ☑ **D.** When you have broken down

113 Hazard warning lights should be used when vehicles are

Mark one answer
- ☑ **A.** Broken down and causing an obstruction
- ☐ **B.** Faulty and moving slowly
- ☐ **C.** Being towed along a road
- ☐ **D.** Reversing into a side road

114 It is important to wear suitable shoes when you are driving. Why is this?

Mark one answer
- ☐ **A.** To prevent wear on the pedals
- ☑ **B.** To maintain control of the pedals
- ☐ **C.** To enable you to adjust your seat
- ☐ **D.** To enable you to walk for assistance if you break down

115 A properly adjusted head restraint will

Mark one answer
- ☐ **A.** Make you more comfortable
- ☑ **B.** Help you to avoid neck injury
- ☐ **C.** Help you to relax
- ☐ **D.** Help you to maintain your driving position

116 What will reduce the risk of neck injury resulting from a collision?

Mark one answer
- ☐ **A.** An air-sprung seat
- ☐ **B.** Anti-lock brakes
- ☐ **C.** A collapsible steering wheel
- ☑ **D.** A properly adjusted head restraint

117 How can you, as a driver, help the environment? *окружающий среде*

Mark three answers

- [x] **A.** By reducing your speed
- [x] **B.** By gentle acceleration
- [ ] **C.** By using leaded fuel
- [ ] **D.** By driving faster
- [ ] **E.** By harsh acceleration
- [x] **F.** By servicing your vehicle properly ✓

118 To help the environment, you can avoid wasting fuel by

Mark three answers

- [x] **A.** Having your vehicle properly serviced ✓
- [x] **B.** Making sure your tyres are correctly inflated
- [x] **C.** Not over-revving in the lower gears
- [ ] **D.** Driving at higher speeds where possible
- [ ] **E.** Keeping an empty roof rack properly fitted
- [ ] **F.** Servicing your vehicle less regularly

119 Why do MOT tests include a strict exhaust emission test?

Mark one answer

- [ ] **A.** To recover the cost of expensive garage equipment
- [x] **B.** To help protect the environment against pollution ✓
- [ ] **C.** To discover which fuel supplier is used the most
- [ ] **D.** To make sure diesel and petrol engines emit the same fumes

120 Which THREE things can you, as a road user, do to help the environment?

Mark three answers

- [x] **A.** Cycle when possible ✓
- [ ] **B.** Drive on under-inflated tyres
- [ ] **C.** Use the choke for as long as possible on a cold engine *дросселе*
- [x] **D.** Have your vehicle properly tuned and serviced ✓
- [x] **E.** Watch the traffic and plan ahead —
- [ ] **F.** Brake as late as possible without skidding

121 As a driver you can cause MORE damage to the environment by

Mark three answers

- [ ] **A.** Choosing a fuel efficient vehicle
- [x] **B.** Making a lot of short journeys
- [ ] **C.** Driving in as high a gear as possible
- [x] **D.** Accelerating as quickly as possible
- [ ] **E.** Having your vehicle regularly serviced
- [x] **F.** Using leaded fuel

122 Motor vehicles can harm the environment. This has resulted in

Mark three answers

- [x] **A.** Air pollution ✓
- [x] **B.** Damage to buildings
- [ ] **C.** Reduced health risks
- [ ] **D.** Improved public transport
- [ ] **E.** Less use of electrical vehicles
- [x] **F.** Using up natural resources

123 To reduce the damage your vehicle causes to the environment you should

Mark three answers

- [ ] **A.** Use narrow side streets
- [x] **B.** Avoid harsh acceleration ✓
- [x] **C.** Brake in good time ✓
- [x] **D.** Anticipate well ahead ✓
- [ ] **E.** Use busy routes

124 You will help the environment if you

Mark one answer

- [ ] **A.** Reduce the tyre pressures
- [ ] **B.** Drive continually using full choke
- [ ] **C.** Accelerate and brake sharply
- [x] **D.** Walk or cycle when you can ✓

125 To help protect the environment you should NOT

Mark one answer

- [x] **A.** Remove your roof rack when unloaded
- [ ] **B.** Use your car for very short journeys ✓
- [ ] **C.** Walk, cycle, or use public transport
- [ ] **D.** Empty the boot of unnecessary weight

126 You service your own vehicle. How should you get rid of the old engine oil?

Mark one answer

- [x] **A.** Take it to a local authority site ✓
- [ ] **B.** Pour it down a drain
- [ ] **C.** Tip it into a hole in the ground
- [ ] **D.** Put it into your dustbin

127 Waste engine oil should be disposed of

Mark one answer

- [ ] **A.** At the local demolition site
- [ ] **B.** Down a water drain
- [x] **C.** At the local authority site ·
- [ ] **D.** On nearby waste land

128 You are carrying two 13-year-old children and their parents in your car. Who is responsible for seeing that the children wear seat belts?

Mark one answer

- [ ] **A.** The children's parents
- [x] **B.** You, the driver ✓
- [ ] **C.** The front-seat passenger
- [ ] **D.** The children

129 You are driving a friend's children home from school. They are both under 14 years old. Who is responsible for making sure they wear a seat belt?

Mark one answer

- [ ] **A.** An adult passenger
- [ ] **B.** The children
- [x] **C.** You, the driver ✓
- [ ] **D.** Your friend

130 Car passengers MUST wear a seat belt if one is available, unless they are

Mark one answer

- [ ] **A.** Under 14 years old
- [ ] **B.** Under 1.5 metres (5 feet) in height
- [ ] **C.** Sitting in the rear seat
- [x] **D.** Exempt for medical reasons

131 Excessive or uneven tyre wear can be caused by faults in which THREE?

Mark three answers

- [ ] **A.** The gearbox
- [x] **B.** The braking system
- [ ] **C.** The accelerator
- [ ] **D.** The exhaust system
- [x] **E.** Wheel alignment ✓ *выравнивание*
- [x] **F.** The suspension ✓

132 You are testing your suspension. You notice that your vehicle keeps bouncing when you press down on the front wing. What does this mean?

Mark one answer

- [ ] **A.** Worn tyres
- [ ] **B.** Tyres under-inflated ✓
- [ ] **C.** Steering wheel not located centrally
- [x] **D.** Worn shock absorbers

133 Which of the following will improve fuel consumption? *потребление*

Mark two answers

- [x] **A.** Reducing your road speed
- [x] **B.** Planning well ahead ✓
- [ ] **C.** Late and harsh braking
- [ ] **D.** Driving in lower gears
- [ ] **E.** Short journeys with a cold engine
- [ ] **F.** Rapid acceleration

134 Which THREE of the following are most likely to waste fuel?

Mark three answers

- [ ] **A.** Reducing your speed
- [x] **B.** Carrying unnecessary weight ✓
- [ ] **C.** Using the wrong grade of fuel ✓
- [x] **D.** Under-inflated tyres
- [ ] **E.** Using different brands of fuel ✓
- [x] **F.** A fitted, empty roof rack ?

135 In which of these containers may you carry petrol in a motor vehicle?

Mark one answer

- [x] **A.**
- [ ] **B.**
- [ ] **C.**
- [ ] **D.**

136 You have a loose filler cap on your diesel fuel tank. This will

Mark two answers

- [x] **A.** Waste fuel and money ✓
- [x] **B.** Make roads slippery for other road users
- [ ] **C.** Improve your vehicle's fuel consumption
- [ ] **D.** Increase the level of exhaust emissions

137 *проливать* To avoid spillage after refuelling, you should make sure that

Mark one answer
- [ ] **A.** Your tank is only ¾ full
- [ ] **B.** You have used a locking filler cap
- [ ] **C.** You check your fuel gauge is working
- [x] **D.** Your filler cap is securely fastened ✓

Mark one answer
- [x] **A.** They give a wider field of vision ✓
- [ ] **B.** They totally cover blind spots
- [ ] **C.** They make it easier to judge the speed of following traffic
- [ ] **D.** They make following traffic look bigger

138 Extra care should be taken when refuelling, because diesel fuel when spilt is

Mark one answer
- [ ] **A.** Sticky
- [ ] **C.** Clear
- [ ] **B.** Odourless
- [x] **D.** Slippery ✓

Одуванчик

142 You cannot see clearly behind when reversing. What should you do?

Mark one answer
- [ ] **A.** Open your window to look behind
- [ ] **B.** Open the door and look behind ✓
- [ ] **C.** Look in the nearside mirror
- [x] **D.** Ask someone to guide you

139 You must NOT sound your horn

Mark one answer
- [ ] **A.** Between 10pm and 6am in a built-up area
- [ ] **B.** At any time in a built-up area
- [x] **C.** Between 11.30pm and 7am in a built-up area ✓
- [ ] **D.** Between 11.30pm and 6am on any road

143 What will cause high fuel consumption?

Mark one answer
- [ ] **A.** Poor steering control
- [ ] **B.** Accelerating around bends
- [ ] **C.** Driving in high gears
- [x] **D.** Harsh braking and accelerating

резкий разгон

140 When should you NOT use your horn in a built-up area?

Mark one answer
- [ ] **A.** Between 8pm and 8am
- [ ] **B.** Between 9pm and dawn
- [ ] **C.** Between dusk and 8am
- [x] **D.** Between 11.30pm and 7am ✓

144 A properly serviced vehicle will give

Mark two answers
- [ ] **A.** Lower insurance premiums
- [ ] **B.** You a refund on your road tax
- [x] **C.** Better fuel economy ✓
- [x] **D.** Cleaner exhaust emissions ✓

141 Why are mirrors on the outside of vehicles often slightly curved (convex)?

выпуклое

выпуклое

145 Driving at 70mph uses more fuel than driving at 50mph by up to

Mark one answer
- [ ] **A.** 10%
- [x] **B.** 30%
- [ ] **C.** 75%
- [ ] **D.** 100%

146 When driving a car fitted with automatic transmission what would you use 'kick down' for?

Mark one answer *mutox - gne oбrou*

☐ **A.** Cruise control
☑ **B.** Quick acceleration
☐ **C.** Slow braking
☐ **D.** Fuel economy

147 When a roof-rack is not in use it should be removed. Why is this?

Mark one answer

☐ **A.** It will affect the suspension
☐ **B.** It is illegal
☐ **C.** It will affect your braking
☑ **D.** It will waste fuel

148 A roof-rack fitted to your car will

Mark one answer

☐ **A.** Reduce fuel consumption
☐ **B.** Improve the road handling
☐ **C.** Make your car go faster
☑ **D.** Increase fuel consumption ✓

149 The pictured vehicle is 'Environmentally Friendly' because it

Mark three answers

☑ **A.** Reduces noise pollution
☐ **B.** Uses diesel fuel
☑ **C.** Uses electricity ✓
☐ **D.** Uses unleaded fuel
☐ **E.** Reduces parking spaces
☑ **F.** Reduces town traffic

150 Supertrams or Light Rapid Transit (LRT) systems are environmentally friendly because

Mark one answer

☐ **A.** They use diesel power
☐ **B.** They use quieter roads
☑ **C.** They use electric power ✓
☐ **D.** They do not operate during rush hour

151 'Red routes' in major cities have been introduced to

Mark one answer

☐ **A.** Raise the speed limits
☑ **B.** Help the traffic flow *Teyb*
☐ **C.** Provide better parking
☐ **D.** Allow lorries to load more freely *cbolgno*

152 To reduce the volume of traffic on the roads you could

Mark three answers

☑ **A.** Use public transport more often ✓
☑ **B.** Share a car when possible ✓
☑ **C.** Walk or cycle on short journeys ✓
☐ **D.** Travel by car at all times
☐ **E.** Use a car with a smaller engine
☐ **F.** Drive in a bus lane

153 In some narrow residential streets you will find a speed limit of

Mark one answer

☑ **A.** 20mph   ☐ **B.** 25mph
☐ **C.** 35mph   ☐ **D.** 40mph

154 Road humps, chicanes, and narrowings are

Mark one answer

- [ ] **A.** Always at major road works
- [ ] **B.** Used to increase traffic speed ✓
- [ ] **C.** At toll-bridge approaches only
- [✓] **D.** Traffic calming measures

155 You enter a road where there are road humps. What should you do?

Mark one answer

- [✓] **A.** Maintain a reduced speed throughout ✓
- [ ] **B.** Accelerate quickly between each one
- [ ] **C.** Always keep to the maximum legal speed
- [ ] **D.** Drive slowly at school times only

156 On your vehicle, where would you find a catalytic converter?

Mark one answer

- [ ] **A.** In the fuel tank
- [ ] **B.** In the air filter
- [ ] **C.** On the cooling system
- [✓] **D.** On the exhaust system

157 Leaded petrol must NOT be used in vehicles fitted with

Mark one answer

- [ ] **A.** A fuel injection system
- [✓] **B.** A catalytic converter
- [ ] **C.** An engine of less than 1,000cc
- [ ] **D.** A stainless steel exhaust

158 New vehicles are fitted with catalytic converters if they use

Mark one answer

- [ ] **A.** Gas power
- [✓] **B.** Unleaded petrol ✓
- [ ] **C.** Leaded petrol
- [ ] **D.** Battery power

159 For which TWO of these may you use hazard warning lights?

Mark two answers

- [✓] **A.** When driving on a motorway, to warn other drivers behind of a hazard ahead
- [ ] **B.** When you are double-parked on a two-way road
- [ ] **C.** When your direction indicators are not working
- [ ] **D.** When warning oncoming traffic that you intend to stop
- [✓] **E.** When your vehicle has broken down and is causing an obstruction ✓

160 Daytime visibility is poor but not seriously reduced. You should switch on

Mark one answer

- [ ] **A.** Headlights and fog light
- [ ] **B.** Front fog lights
- [✓] **C.** Dipped headlights
- [ ] **D.** Rear fog lights

161 Why are vehicles fitted with rear fog lights?

Mark one answer

- [ ] **A.** To be seen when driving at high speed
- [ ] **B.** To use if broken down in a dangerous position
- [✓] **C.** To make them more visible in thick fog ✓
- [ ] **D.** To warn drivers following closely to drop back

162 Your vehicle is fitted with anti-lock brakes. To stop quickly in an emergency you should

Mark one answer NI

- **A.** Brake firmly and pump the brake pedal on and off ✓
- ☑ **B.** Brake rapidly and firmly without releasing the brake pedal
- **C.** Brake gently and pump the brake pedal on and off
- **D.** Brake rapidly once, and immediately release the brake pedal

163 Your car is fitted with anti-lock brakes. You need to stop in an emergency. You should

Mark one answer NI

- **A.** Brake normally and avoid turning the steering wheel
- ☑ **B.** Press the brake pedal rapidly and firmly until you have stopped ✓
- **C.** Keep pushing and releasing the foot brake quickly to prevent skidding _занос_
- **D.** Apply the handbrake to reduce the stopping distance

164 You are driving a vehicle fitted with anti-lock brakes. You need to stop in an emergency. You should apply the footbrake

Mark one answer NI

- **A.** Slowly and gently
- **B.** Slowly but firmly
- **C.** Rapidly and gently
- ☑ **D.** Rapidly and firmly ✓

165 Anti-lock brakes reduce the chances of a skid occurring particularly when

Mark one answer

- **A.** Driving down steep hills
- **B.** Braking during normal driving
- ☑ **C.** Braking in an emergency ·
- **D.** Driving on good road surfaces

166 Your vehicle has anti-lock brakes, but they may not always prevent skidding. This is most likely to happen when driving

Mark two answers

- **A.** In foggy conditions
- ☑ **B.** On surface water ✓
- ☑ **C.** On loose road surfaces _сыпучи_
- **D.** On dry tarmac _чугунн_
- **E.** At night on unlit roads

167 Anti-lock brakes prevent wheels from locking. This means the tyres are less likely to

Mark one answer

- **A.** Aquaplane
- ☑ **B.** Skid
- **C.** Puncture
- **D.** Wear

168 Anti-lock brakes are most effective when you

Mark one answer NI

- [ ] **A.** Keep pumping the foot brake to prevent skidding
- [ ] **B.** Brake normally, but grip the steering wheel tightly
- [x] **C.** Brake rapidly and firmly until you have slowed down ✓
- [ ] **D.** Apply the handbrake to reduce the stopping distance

169 Vehicles fitted with anti-lock brakes

Mark one answer

- [ ] **A.** Are impossible to skid
- [x] **B.** Can be steered while you are braking
- [ ] **C.** Accelerate much faster
- [ ] **D.** Are not fitted with a handbrake

170 Anti-lock brakes may not work as effectively if the road surface is

Mark two answers

- [ ] **A.** Dry
- [x] **B.** Loose ✓
- [x] **C.** Wet ✓
- [ ] **D.** Good
- [ ] **E.** Firm

171 Anti-lock brakes are of most use when you are

Mark one answer

- [ ] **A.** Braking gently
- [ ] **B.** Driving on worn tyres
- [x] **C.** Braking excessively
- [ ] **D.** Driving normally

172 Driving a vehicle fitted with anti-lock brakes allows you to

Mark one answer

- [ ] **A.** Brake harder because it is impossible to skid
- [ ] **B.** Drive at higher speeds
- [x] **C.** Steer and brake at the same time ✓
- [ ] **D.** Pay less attention to the road ahead

173 When would an anti-lock braking system start to work?

Mark one answer

- [ ] **A.** After the parking brake has been applied
- [ ] **B.** Whenever pressure on the brake pedal is applied
- [x] **C.** Just as the wheels are about to lock
- [ ] **D.** When the normal braking system fails to operate

174 Anti-lock brakes will take effect when

Mark one answer

- [ ] **A.** You do not brake quickly enough
- [x] **B.** Excessive brake pressure has been applied
- [ ] **C.** You have not seen a hazard ahead
- [ ] **D.** Speeding on slippery road surfaces

175 Anti-lock brakes can greatly assist with

Mark one answer

- [ ] **A.** A higher cruising speed
- [x] **B.** Steering control when braking ✓
- [ ] **C.** Control when accelerating
- [ ] **D.** Motorway driving

176 You are on a good, dry road surface and your vehicle has good brakes and tyres. What is the overall stopping distance at 40mph?

Mark one answer
- **A.** 23 metres (75 feet)
- ☑ **B.** 36 metres (118 feet) ✓
- **C.** 53 metres (174 feet)
- **D.** 96 metres (315 feet)

177 You are on a good, dry road surface. Your vehicle has good brakes and tyres. What is the braking distance at 50mph?

Mark one answer
- ☑ **A.** 38 metres (125 feet)
- **B.** 14 metres (46 feet)
- **C.** 24 metres (79 feet)
- **D.** 55 metres (180 feet) ✓

178 Braking hard at speed on a sharp bend can make your vehicle

Mark one answer
- **A.** More stable
- ☑ **B.** Unstable ✓
- **C.** Stall
- **D.** Corner safely

179 What is the shortest stopping distance at 70mph?

Mark one answer
- **A.** 53 metres (174 feet)
- **B.** 60 metres (197 feet)
- **C.** 73 metres (240 feet)
- ☑ **D.** 96 metres (315 feet)

180 You are travelling at 50mph on a good, dry road. What is your shortest overall stopping distance?

Mark one answer
- **A.** 36 metres (118 feet)
- ☑ **B.** 53 metres (174 feet)
- **C.** 75 metres (245 feet)
- **D.** 96 metres (315 feet)

181 What is the shortest overall stopping distance on a dry road from 60mph?

Mark one answer
- **A.** 53 metres (174 feet)
- **B.** 58 metres (190 feet)
- ☑ **C.** 73 metres (240 feet)
- **D.** 96 metres (315 feet)

182 When driving in fog, which of the following are correct?

Mark three answers
- ☑ **A.** Use dipped headlights ✓
- **B.** Use headlamps on full beam
- ☑ **C.** Allow more time for your journey ✓
- **D.** Keep close to the car in front
- ☑ **E.** Slow down ✓
- **F.** Use side lights only

183 You are on a fast, open road in good conditions. For safety, the distance between you and the vehicle in front should be

Mark one answer
- ☑ **A.** A two-second time gap ✓
- ☐ **B.** One car length
- ☐ **C.** 2 metres (6 feet 6 inches)
- ☐ **D.** Two car lengths

184 The two-second rule helps you to

Mark one answer
- ☑ **A.** Keep a safe distance from the car in front ✓
- ☐ **B.** Keep the correct distance from the kerb
- ☐ **C.** Check your blind spot
- ☐ **D.** Check your mirrors

185 Your overall stopping distance will be much longer when driving

Mark one answer
- ☑ **A.** In the rain ✓
- ☐ **B.** In fog
- ☐ **C.** At night
- ☐ **D.** In strong winds

186 What is the main reason why your stopping distance is longer after heavy rain?

Mark one answer
- ☐ **A.** You may not be able to see large puddles
- ☐ **B.** The brakes will be cold because they are wet
- ☑ **C.** Your tyres will have less grip on the road ✓
- ☐ **D.** Water on the windscreen will blur your view of the road ahead

187 What is the most common cause of skidding?

Mark one answer
- ☐ **A.** Worn tyres
- ☑ **B.** Driver error ✓
- ☐ **C.** Other vehicles
- ☐ **D.** Pedestrians

188 When braking hard in a straight line, the weight of the vehicle will shift onto the

Mark one answer
- ☑ **A.** Front wheels ✓
- ☐ **B.** Rear wheels
- ☐ **C.** Left wheels
- ☐ **D.** Right wheels

189 You are driving in heavy rain. Your steering suddenly becomes very light. You should

Mark one answer
- ☐ **A.** Steer towards the side of the road
- ☐ **B.** Apply gentle acceleration
- ☐ **C.** Brake firmly to reduce speed
- ☑ **D.** Ease off the accelerator ✓

190 You have driven through a flood. What is the first thing you should do?

Mark one answer
- **A.** Stop and check the tyres
- **B.** Stop and dry the brakes ✓
- **C.** Switch on your windscreen wipers
- ✓ **D.** Test your brakes

191 You are driving along a country road. You see this sign. AFTER dealing safely with the hazard you should always

Ford

Mark one answer
- **A.** Check your tyre pressures
- **B.** Switch on your hazard warning lights
- **C.** Accelerate briskly
- ✓ **D.** Test your brakes

192 Braking distances on ice can be

Mark one answer
- **A.** Twice the normal distance
- **B.** Five times the normal distance
- **C.** Seven times the normal distance
- ✓ **D.** Ten times the normal distance

193 Freezing conditions will affect the distance it takes you to come to a stop. You should expect stopping distances to increase by up to

Mark one answer
- **A.** Two times
- **B.** Five times
- **C.** Three times
- ✓ **D.** Ten times

194 When driving in icy conditions, the steering becomes light because the tyres

Mark one answer
- **A.** Have more grip on the road
- **B.** Are too soft
- **C.** Are too hard
- ✓ **D.** Have less grip on the road

195 You are driving on an icy road. How can you avoid wheelspin?

Mark one answer
- ✓ **A.** Drive at a slow speed in as high a gear as possible ✓
- **B.** Use the handbrake if the wheels start to slip
- **C.** Brake gently and repeatedly
- **D.** Drive in a low gear at all times

196 Skidding is mainly caused by

Mark one answer
- **A.** The weather
- ✓ **B.** The driver
- **C.** The vehicle
- **D.** The road

197 How can you avoid wheelspin when driving in freezing conditions?

Mark one answer
- [ ] **A.** Stay in first gear all the time
- [ ] **B.** Put on your handbrake if the wheels begin to slip
- [x] **C.** Drive in as high a gear as possible
- [ ] **D.** Allow the vehicle to coast in neutral

198 You are driving in freezing conditions. What should you do when approaching a sharp bend?

Mark two answers
- [x] **A.** Slow down before you reach the bend
- [ ] **B.** Gently apply your handbrake
- [ ] **C.** Firmly use your footbrake
- [ ] **D.** Coast into the bend
- [x] **E.** Avoid sudden steering movements

199 You are turning left on a slippery road. The back of your vehicle slides to the right. You should

Mark one answer
- [ ] **A.** Brake firmly and not turn the steering wheel
- [ ] **B.** Steer carefully to the left
- [x] **C.** Steer carefully to the right
- [ ] **D.** Brake firmly and steer to the left

200 You are braking on a wet road. Your vehicle begins to skid. Your vehicle does not have anti-lock brakes. What is the FIRST thing you should do?

Mark one answer
- [ ] **A.** Quickly pull up the handbrake
- [x] **B.** Release the footbrake fully
- [ ] **C.** Push harder on the brake pedal
- [ ] **D.** Gently use the accelerator

201 How can you tell when you are driving over black ice?

Mark one answer
- [ ] **A.** It is easier to brake
- [ ] **B.** The noise from your tyres sounds louder
- [ ] **C.** You see black ice on the road
- [x] **D.** Your steering feels light

202 Coasting the vehicle

Mark one answer
- [ ] **A.** Improves the driver's control
- [ ] **B.** Makes steering easier
- [x] **C.** Reduces the driver's control
- [ ] **D.** Uses more fuel

203 Before starting a journey in freezing weather you should clear ice and snow from your vehicle's

Mark four answers
- [ ] **A.** Aerial
- [x] **B.** Windows
- [ ] **C.** Bumper
- [x] **D.** Lights
- [x] **E.** Mirrors
- [x] **F.** Number plates

204 You are driving in falling snow. Your wipers are not clearing the windscreen. You should

Mark one answer
- [ ] **A.** Set the windscreen demister to cool
- [x] **B.** Be prepared to clear the windscreen by hand ✓
- [ ] **C.** Use the windscreen washers
- [ ] **D.** Partly open the front windows

205 When driving on snow it is best to keep in as high a gear as possible. Why is this?

Mark one answer
- [ ] **A.** To help you slow down quickly when you brake
- [ ] **B.** So that the wheelspin does not cause your engine to run too fast
- [ ] **C.** To leave a lower gear available in case of wheelspin
- [x] **D.** To help to prevent wheelspin ✓

206 You are trying to move off on snow. You should use

Mark one answer
- [ ] **A.** The lowest gear you can
- [x] **B.** The highest gear you can
- [ ] **C.** A high engine speed
- [ ] **D.** The handbrake and footbrake together

207 When driving in falling snow you should

Mark one answer
- [ ] **A.** Brake firmly and quickly
- [ ] **B.** Be ready to steer sharply
- [ ] **C.** Use sidelights only
- [x] **D.** Brake gently in plenty of time ✓

208 The MAIN benefit of having four-wheel drive is to improve

Mark one answer
- [x] **A.** Road holding ✓
- [ ] **B.** Fuel consumption
- [ ] **C.** Stopping distances
- [ ] **D.** Passenger comfort

209 When driving in fog in daylight you should use

Mark one answer
- [ ] **A.** Sidelights
- [ ] **B.** Full beam headlights
- [ ] **C.** Hazard lights
- [x] **D.** Dipped headlights ✓

210 You are at a junction with limited visibility. You should

Mark one answer
- [ ] **A.** Inch forward, looking to the right
- [ ] **B.** Inch forward, looking to the left
- [x] **C.** Inch forward, looking both ways ✓
- [ ] **D.** Be ready to move off quickly

211 In very hot weather the road surface can get soft. Which TWO of the following will be affected most?

Mark two answers
- **A.** The suspension
- ☑ **B.** The steering
- ☑ **C.** The braking
- **D.** The windscreen

212 Where are you most likely to be affected by a sidewind?

Mark one answer
- **A.** On a narrow country lane
- ☑ **B.** On an open stretch of road
- **C.** On a busy stretch of road
- **D.** On a long, straight road ✓

213 In windy conditions you need to take extra care when

Mark one answer
- **A.** Using the brakes ✓
- **B.** Making a hill start
- **C.** Turning into a narrow road
- ☑ **D.** Passing pedal cyclists

214 Your indicators may be difficult to see in bright sunlight. What should you do?

Mark one answer
- **A.** Put your indicator on earlier
- ☑ **B.** Give an arm signal as well as using your indicator ✓
- **C.** Touch the brake several times to show the stop lamps
- **D.** Turn as quickly as you can

215 You are about to go down a steep hill. To control the speed of your vehicle you should

Mark one answer
- **A.** Select a high gear and use the brakes carefully
- **B.** Select a high gear and use the brakes firmly
- ☑ **C.** Select a low gear and use the brakes carefully
- **D.** Select a low gear and avoid using the brakes ✓

216 You are on a long, downhill slope. What should you do to help control the speed of your vehicle?

Mark one answer
- **A.** Select neutral
- ☑ **B.** Select a lower gear ✓
- **C.** Grip the handbrake firmly
- **D.** Apply the parking brake gently

217 How can you use the engine of your vehicle as a brake?

Mark one answer
- ☑ **A.** By changing to a lower gear ✓
- **B.** By selecting reverse gear
- **C.** By changing to a higher gear
- **D.** By selecting neutral gear

218 You wish to park facing DOWNHILL. Which TWO of the following should you do?

Mark two answers

- ☑ **A.** Turn the steering wheel towards the kerb
- ☐ **B.** Park close to the bumper of another car
- ☐ **C.** Park with two wheels on the kerb
- ☑ **D.** Put the handbrake on firmly ✓
- ☐ **E.** Turn the steering wheel away from the kerb

219 You are driving in a built-up area. You approach a speed hump. You should

Mark one answer

- ☐ **A.** Move across to the left-hand side of the road
- ☐ **B.** Wait for any pedestrians to cross
- ☑ **C.** Slow your vehicle right down ✓
- ☐ **D.** Stop and check both pavements

220 When approaching a right-hand bend you should keep well to the left. Why is this?

Mark one answer

- ☑ **A.** To improve your view of the road
- ☐ **B.** To overcome the effect of the road's slope
- ☐ **C.** To let faster traffic from behind overtake
- ☐ **D.** To be positioned safely if the vehicle skids ✓

221 You are coming up to a right-hand bend. You should

Mark one answer

- ☐ **A.** Keep well to the left as it makes the bend faster
- ☑ **B.** Keep well to the left for a better view around the bend ✓
- ☐ **C.** Keep well to the right to avoid anything in the gutter
- ☐ **D.** Keep well to the right to make the bend less sharp

222 You should not overtake when

Mark three answers

- ☑ **A.** Intending to turn left shortly afterwards
- ☐ **B.** In a one-way street
- ☑ **C.** Approaching a junction ✓
- ☐ **D.** Driving up a long hill
- ☑ **E.** The view ahead is blocked ✓

223 You see this sign on the rear of a slow-moving lorry that you want to pass. It is travelling in the middle lane of a three-lane motorway. You should

Mark one answer
- [ ] **A.** Cautiously approach the lorry then pass on either side
- [ ] **B.** Follow the lorry until you can leave the motorway
- [ ] **C.** Wait on the hard shoulder until the lorry has stopped
- [x] **D.** Approach with care and keep to the left of the lorry ✓

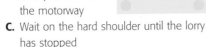

224 Where would you expect to see these markers?

Mark two answers
- [ ] **A.** On a motorway sign
- [ ] **B.** At the entrance to a narrow bridge
- [x] **C.** On a large goods vehicle ✓
- [x] **D.** On a builder's skip placed on the road ✓

225 What does this signal, from a police officer, mean to oncoming traffic?

Mark one answer
- [ ] **A.** Go ahead
- [x] **B.** Stop ✓
- [ ] **C.** Turn left
- [ ] **D.** Turn right

226 What is the main hazard shown in this picture?

Mark one answer
- [ ] **A.** Vehicles turning right
- [ ] **B.** Vehicles doing U-turns
- [x] **C.** The cyclist crossing the road ✓
- [ ] **D.** Parked cars around the corner

227 Which road user has caused a hazard?

Mark one answer
- [x] **A.** The parked car (arrowed A) ✓
- [ ] **B.** The pedestrian waiting to cross (arrowed B)
- [ ] **C.** The moving car (arrowed C)
- [ ] **D.** The car turning (arrowed D)

228 What should the driver of the car approaching the crossing do?

Mark one answer

☐ **A.** Continue at the same speed
☐ **B.** Sound the horn
☐ **C.** Drive through quickly
☑ **D.** Slow down and get ready to stop ✓

229 What should the driver of the red car (arrowed) do?

Mark one answer

☐ **A.** Wave on the pedestrians who are waiting to cross
☑ **B.** Wait for the pedestrian in the road to cross ✓
☐ **C.** Quickly drive behind the pedestrian in the road
☐ **D.** Tell the pedestrian in the road she should not have crossed

230 What THREE things should the driver of the grey car (arrowed) be especially aware of?

Mark three answers

☑ **A.** Pedestrians stepping out between cars ✓
☐ **B.** Other cars behind the grey car
☑ **C.** Doors opening on parked cars ✓
☐ **D.** The bumpy road surface
☑ **E.** Cars leaving parking spaces ✓
☐ **F.** Empty parking spaces

231 What should the driver of the red car (arrowed) do?

Mark one answer

☐ **A.** Sound the horn to tell other drivers where he is
☐ **B.** Squeeze through the gap
☐ **C.** Wave the driver of the white car to go on
☑ **D.** Wait until the car blocking the way has moved ✓

232 What should the driver of the grey car (arrowed) do?

Mark one answer

- ☑ **A.** Cross if the way is clear ✓
- ☐ **B.** Reverse out of the box junction
- ☐ **C.** Wait in the same place until the lights are green
- ☐ **D.** Wait until the lights are red then cross

233 What should the driver of a car coming up to this level crossing do?

Mark one answer

- ☐ **A.** Drive through quickly
- ☐ **B.** Drive through carefully
- ☑ **C.** Stop before the barrier ✓
- ☐ **D.** Switch on hazard warning lights

234 What are TWO main hazards a driver should be aware of when driving along this street?

Mark two answers

- ☐ **A.** Glare from the sun
- ☑ **B.** Car doors opening suddenly ✓
- ☐ **C.** Lack of road markings
- ☐ **D.** The headlights on parked cars being switched on
- ☐ **E.** Large goods vehicles
- ☑ **F.** Children running out from between vehicles ✓

235 What is the main hazard a driver should be aware of when following this cyclist?

Mark one answer

- ☐ **A.** The cyclist may move into the left and dismount
- ☑ **B.** The cyclist may swerve out into the road
- ☐ **C.** The contents of the cyclist's carrier may fall onto the road
- ☐ **D.** The cyclist may wish to turn right at the end of the road ✓

236 The driver of which car has caused a hazard?

Mark one answer

- [ ] **A.** Glare from the sun may affect the driver's vision
- [ ] **B.** The black car may stop suddenly
- [x] **C.** The bus may move out into the road ✓
- [ ] **D.** Oncoming vehicles will assume the driver is turning right

Mark one answer

- [x] **A.** Car A. ✓
- [ ] **B.** Car B.
- [ ] **C.** Car C.
- [ ] **D.** Car D.

---

237 You think the driver of the vehicle in front has forgotten to cancel the right indicator. You should

Mark one answer

- [ ] **A.** Flash your lights to alert the driver
- [ ] **B.** Sound your horn before overtaking
- [ ] **C.** Overtake on the left if there is room
- [x] **D.** Stay behind and not overtake ✓

---

238 What is the main hazard the driver of the red car (arrowed) should be most aware of?

239 In heavy motorway traffic you are being followed closely by the vehicle behind. How can you lower the risk of an accident?

Mark one answer

- [x] **A.** Increase your distance from the vehicle in front ✓
- [ ] **B.** Tap your foot on the brake pedal
- [ ] **C.** Switch on your hazard lights
- [ ] **D.** Move onto the hard shoulder and stop

---

240 You are driving along this dual carriageway. Why may you need to slow down ?

Mark one answer
- **A.** There is a broken white line in the centre
- ☑ **C.** There are roadworks ahead of you ✓
- **B.** There are solid white lines either side
- **D.** There are no footpaths

241 What does the solid white line at the side of the road indicate?

Mark one answer
- **A.** Traffic lights ahead
- ☑ **B.** Edge of the carriageway ✓
- **C.** Footpath on the left
- **D.** Cycle path

242 You see this sign ahead. You should expect the road to

Mark one answer
- **A.** Go steeply uphill
- **B.** Go steeply downhill
- ☑ **C.** Bend sharply to the left ✓
- **D.** Bend sharply to the right

243 You are approaching this cyclist. You should

Mark one answer
- **A.** Overtake before the cyclist gets to the junction
- **B.** Flash your headlights at the cyclist
- ☑ **C.** Slow down and allow the cyclist to turn ✓
- **D.** Overtake the cyclist on the left-hand side

244 You have just been overtaken by this motorcyclist who is cutting in sharply. You should

Mark one answer
- **A.** Sound the horn
- **B.** Brake firmly
- ☑ **C.** Keep a safe gap ✓
- **D.** Remember to flash your lights

245 Why must you take extra care when turning right at this junction?

Mark one answer

- [ ] **A.** Road surface is poor
- [ ] **B.** Footpaths are narrow
- [ ] **C.** Road markings are faint
- [x] **D.** There is reduced visibility ✓

 246 What is the main hazard in this picture?

Mark one answer

- [x] **A.** The pedestrian ✓
- [ ] **B.** The parked cars
- [ ] **C.** The junction on the left
- [ ] **D.** The driveway on the left

 247 You are driving towards this parked lorry. What is the first hazard you should be aware of?

Mark one answer

- [ ] **A.** The lorry moving off
- [ ] **B.** The narrowing road
- [x] **C.** The pedestrian crossing ✓
- [ ] **D.** The vehicles ahead

248 This yellow sign on a vehicle indicates this is

Mark one answer

- [ ] **A.** A vehicle broken down
- [x] **B.** A school bus ✓
- [ ] **C.** An ice cream van
- [ ] **D.** A private ambulance

249 You are driving towards this level crossing. What would be the first warning of an approaching train?

Mark one answer

- [ ] **A.** Both half barriers down
- [x] **B.** A steady amber light —
- [ ] **C.** One half barrier down
- [ ] **D.** Twin flashing red lights —

Сначала горит желтый, потом мигает красный...

250 You are driving along this motorway. It is raining. When following this lorry you should

Mark two answers
- [ ] **A.** Allow at least a two-second gap
- [ ] **B.** Move left and drive on the hard shoulder
- [x] **C.** Allow at least a four-second gap ✓
- [x] **D.** Be aware of spray reducing your vision ✓
- [ ] **E.** Move right and stay in the right-hand lane

251 You are behind this cyclist. When the traffic lights change, what should you do?

Mark one answer
- [ ] **A.** Try to move off before the cyclist
- [x] **B.** Allow the cyclist time and room ✓
- [ ] **C.** Turn right but give the cyclist room
- [ ] **D.** Tap your horn and drive through first

252 You are driving towards this left-hand bend. What dangers should you be aware of?

Mark one answer
- [ ] **A.** A vehicle overtaking you
- [ ] **B.** No white lines in the centre of the road
- [ ] **C.** No sign to warn you of the bend
- [x] **D.** Pedestrians walking towards you ✓

253 When approaching this bridge you should give way to

Mark one answer
- [ ] **A.** Bicycles
- [x] **B.** Buses ✓
- [ ] **C.** Motorcycles
- [ ] **D.** Cars

254 What type of vehicle could you expect to meet in the middle of the road?

Mark one answer
- [x] **A.** Lorry ✓
- [ ] **B.** Bicycle
- [ ] **C.** Car
- [ ] **D.** Motorcycle

255 As the driver of this vehicle, why should you slow down?

Mark two answers

- ☑ **A.** Because of the bend
- ☐ **B.** Because it's hard to see to the right
- ☐ **C.** Because of approaching trains
- ☐ **D.** Because of animals crossing
- ☑ **E.** Because of the level crossing ✓

256 While driving, you see this sign ahead. You should

Mark one answer

- ☐ **A.** Stop at the sign
- ☑ **B.** Slow, but continue around the bend
- ☐ **C.** Slow to a crawl and continue
- ☐ **D.** Stop and look for open farm gates

257 Why should the junction on the left be kept clear?

Mark one answer

- ☑ **A.** To allow vehicles to enter and emerge ✓
- ☐ **B.** To allow the bus to reverse
- ☐ **C.** To allow vehicles to make a 'U' turn
- ☐ **D.** To allow vehicles to park

258 What is the first hazard shown in this picture?

Mark one answer

- ☐ **A.** Standing traffic
- ☐ **B.** Oncoming traffic
- ☑ **C.** Junction on the left ✓
- ☐ **D.** Pedestrians

259 You are driving in the left lane but want to turn right at the traffic lights. You should

Mark one answer

- [ ] **A.** Check your mirrors, signal and move to the right
- [ ] **B.** Weave into the middle and then to the right lane
- [ ] **C.** Drive up to the lights then turn right
- [x] **D.** Stay in your lane and find another way back

260 When the traffic lights change to green the white car should

Mark one answer

- [x] **A.** Wait for the cyclist to pull away
- [ ] **B.** Move off quickly and turn in front of the cyclist
- [ ] **C.** Move close up to the cyclist to beat the lights
- [ ] **D.** Sound the horn to warn the cyclist

261 You intend to turn left at the traffic lights. Just before turning you should

Mark one answer

- [ ] **A.** Check your right mirror
- [ ] **B.** Move close up to the white car
- [ ] **C.** Straddle the lanes
- [x] **D.** Check for bicycles on your left

262 You should reduce your speed when driving along this road because

Mark one answer

- [x] **A.** There is a staggered junction ahead
- [ ] **B.** There is a low bridge ahead
- [ ] **C.** There is a change in the road surface
- [ ] **D.** The road ahead narrows

263 An approaching motorcyclist is easier to see when

Mark three answers
- ☑ **A.** The rider is wearing bright clothing ✓
- ☑ **B.** The rider has a white helmet ✓
- ☑ **C.** The headlight is on ✓
- ☐ **D.** The motorcycle is moving slowly
- ☐ **E.** The motorcycle is moving quickly
- ☐ **F.** The rider has a passenger

Mark two answers
- ☑ **A.** Be wary of cars on your right cutting in
- ☐ **B.** Accelerate past the vehicles in the left lane
- ☐ **C.** Pull up on the left-hand verge
- ☐ **D.** Move across and continue in the right-hand lane
- ☑ **E.** Slow down keeping a safe separation distance ✓

264 You are driving at 60mph. As you approach this hazard you should

Mark one answer
- ☐ **A.** Maintain your speed
- ☑ **B.** Reduce your speed ✓
- ☐ **C.** Take the next right turn
- ☐ **D.** Take the next left turn

265 The traffic ahead of you in the left lane is slowing. You should

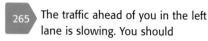

266 What might you expect to happen in this situation?

Mark one answer
- ☐ **A.** Traffic will move into the right-hand lane
- ☐ **B.** Traffic speed will increase
- ☑ **C.** Traffic will move into the left-hand lane ✓
- ☐ **D.** Traffic will not need to change position

267 You are driving on a road with several lanes. You see these signs above the lanes. What do they mean?

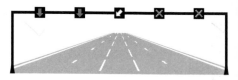

Mark one answer
- [ ] **A.** The two right lanes are open
- [x] **B.** The two left lanes are open ✓
- [ ] **C.** Traffic in the left lanes should stop
- [ ] **D.** Traffic in the right lanes should stop

Mark one answer
- [ ] **A.** During rush hour only
- [ ] **B.** Only when the area is busy
- [ ] **C.** When turning right only
- [x] **D.** At all times ✓

268 At this blind junction you must stop

Mark one answer
- [x] **A.** Behind the line, then edge forward to see clearly
- [ ] **B.** Beyond the line at a point where you can see clearly ✓
- [ ] **C.** Only if there is traffic on the main road
- [ ] **D.** Only if you are turning to the right

269 When must you stop at this junction?

270 As a provisional licence holder, you must not drive a motor car

Mark two answers
- [ ] **A.** At more than 50mph
- [x] **B.** On your own ✓
- [x] **C.** On the motorway ✓
- [ ] **D.** Under the age of 18 years of age at night
- [ ] **E.** With passengers in the rear seats

271 To drive you MUST be able to read a number plate from what distance?

Mark one answer
- [ ] **A.** 10 metres (32 feet)
- [ ] **B.** 15 metres (50 feet)
- [x] **C.** 20.5 metres (67 feet) ✓
- [ ] **D.** 25.5 metres (84 feet)

272 A driver can only read a number plate at the required distance with glasses on. The glasses should be worn

Mark one answer
- [x] **A.** All the time when driving ✓
- [ ] **B.** Only when driving long distances
- [ ] **C.** Only when reversing
- [ ] **D.** Only in poor visibility

273 You are about to drive home. You cannot find the glasses you need to wear when driving. You should

Mark one answer

- **A.** Drive home slowly, keeping to quiet roads
- **B.** Borrow a friend's glasses and drive home
- **C.** Drive home at night, so that the lights will help you
- ✓ **D.** Find a way of getting home without driving ✓

274 You MUST wear glasses or contact lenses when driving on public roads if

Mark one answer

- **A.** You are the holder of an orange badge
- **B.** You cannot read a vehicle number plate from a distance of 36 metres (120 feet) without them
- **C.** There is an eyesight problem in your family
- ✓ **D.** You cannot read a vehicle number plate from a distance of 20.5 metres (67 feet) without them ✓

275 As a driver you find that your eyesight has become very poor. Your optician says he cannot help you. The law says that you should tell

Mark one answer

- ✓ **A.** The licensing authority
- **B.** Your own doctor ✓
- **C.** The local police station
- **D.** Another optician

276 You find that you need glasses to read vehicle number plates. When MUST you wear them?

Mark one answer

- **A.** Only in bad weather conditions
- ✓ **B.** At all times when driving ✓
- **C.** Only when you think it necessary
- **D.** Only in bad light or at night time

277 After passing your driving test, you suffer from ill health. This affects your driving. You MUST

Mark one answer

- **A.** Inform your local police station
- **B.** Get on as best you can
- **C.** Not inform anyone as you hold a full licence
- ✓ **D.** Inform the licensing authority ✓

278 Which THREE result from drinking alcohol and driving?

Mark three answers

- ✓ **A.** Less control ✓
- ✓ **B.** A false sense of confidence ✓
- **C.** Faster reactions
- ✓ **D.** Poor judgement of speed ✓
- **E.** Greater awareness of danger

279 Which THREE of these are likely effects of drinking alcohol on driving?

Mark three answers

- ☑ **A.** Reduced co-ordination ✓
- ☑ **B.** Increased confidence ✓
- ☑ **C.** Poor judgement ✓
- ☐ **D.** Increased concentration
- ☐ **E.** Faster reactions
- ☐ **F.** Colour blindness

280 Drinking any amount of alcohol is likely to

Mark three answers

- ☑ **A.** Slow down your reactions to hazards ✓
- ☐ **B.** Increase the speed of your reactions
- ☑ **C.** Worsen your judgement of speed ✓
- ☐ **D.** Improve your awareness of danger
- ☑ **E.** Give a false sense of confidence ✓

281 You are invited to a pub lunch. You know that you will have to drive in the evening. What is your best course of action?

Mark one answer

- ☐ **A.** Avoid mixing your alcoholic drinks
- ☑ **B.** Not drink any alcohol at all ✓
- ☐ **C.** Have some milk before drinking alcohol
- ☐ **D.** Eat a hot meal with your alcoholic drinks —

282 What else can seriously affect your concentration when driving, other than alcoholic drinks?

Mark three answers

- ☑ **A.** Drugs ✓
- ☑ **B.** Tiredness ✓
- ☐ **C.** Tinted windows
- ☐ **D.** Contact lenses
- ☑ **E.** Loud music ✓

283 How does alcohol affect your driving?

Mark one answer

- ☐ **A.** It speeds up your reactions
- ☐ **B.** It increases your awareness
- ☐ **C.** It improves your co-ordination
- ☑ **D.** It reduces your concentration ✓

284 After drinking alcohol heavily you should not drive the following day. Why is this?

Mark two answers

- ☑ **A.** You may still be over the legal limit —
- ☐ **B.** Your concentration will not be badly affected
- ☐ **C.** You will be well under the legal limit
- ☑ **D.** Your concentration may still be badly affected ✓

285 You have been convicted of driving whilst unfit through drink or drugs. You will find this is likely to cause the cost of one of the following to rise considerably. Which one?

Mark one answer

- [ ] **A.** Road fund licence
- [x] **B.** Insurance premiums ✓
- [ ] **C.** Vehicle test certificate
- [ ] **D.** Driving licence

286 What advice should you give to a driver who has had a few alcoholic drinks at a party?

Mark one answer

- [ ] **A.** Have a strong cup of coffee and then drive home
- [ ] **B.** Drive home carefully and slowly
- [x] **C.** Go home by public transport ✓
- [ ] **D.** Wait a short while and then drive home

287 You go to a social event and need to drive a short time after. What precaution should you take?

Mark one answer

- [ ] **A.** Avoid drinking alcohol on an empty stomach
- [ ] **B.** Drink plenty of coffee after drinking alcohol
- [x] **C.** Avoid drinking alcohol completely ✓
- [ ] **D.** Drink plenty of milk before drinking alcohol

288 It is eight hours since you last had an alcoholic drink. Which of the following applies?

Mark two answers

- [ ] **A.** You will certainly be under the legal limit
- [ ] **B.** You will have no alcohol in your system
- [x] **C.** You may still be unfit to drive ✓
- [x] **D.** You may still be over the legal limit

289 Your doctor has given you a course of medicine. Why should you ask if it is OK to drive?

Mark one answer

- [ ] **A.** Drugs make you a better driver by quickening your reactions
- [ ] **B.** You will have to let your insurance company know about the medicine
- [x] **C.** Some types of medicine can cause your reactions to slow down ✓
- [ ] **D.** The medicine you take may affect your hearing

290 You have been taking medicine for a few days which made you feel drowsy. Today you feel better but still need to take the medicine. You should only drive

Mark one answer

- [ ] **A.** If your journey is necessary
- [ ] **B.** At night on quiet roads
- [ ] **C.** If someone goes with you
- [x] **D.** After checking with your doctor ✓

291 You are about to return home from holiday when you become ill. A doctor prescribes drugs which are likely to affect your driving. You should

Mark one answer
- **A.** Drive only if someone is with you
- **B.** Avoid driving on motorways
- ☑ **C.** Not drive yourself ✓
- **D.** Never drive at more than 30mph

292 During periods of illness your ability to drive may be impaired. You MUST

Mark two answers
- **A.** See your doctor each time before you drive
- **B.** Only take smaller doses of any medicines
- ☑ **C.** Be medically fit to drive
- ☑ **D.** Not drive after taking certain medicines ✓
- **E.** Take all your medicines with you when you drive

293 You are not sure if your cough medicine will affect your driving. What TWO things could you do?

Mark two answers
- ☑ **A.** Ask your doctor ✓
- ☑ **B.** Check the medicine label ✓
- **C.** Drive if you feel alright
- **D.** Ask a friend or relative for advice

294 You take some cough medicine given to you by a friend. What should you do before driving?

Mark one answer
- **A.** Ask your friend if taking the medicine affected their driving
- **B.** Drink some strong coffee one hour before driving
- ☑ **C.** Check the label to see if the medicine will affect your driving ✓
- **D.** Drive a short distance to see if the medicine is affecting your driving

295 You have taken medication that may make you feel drowsy. Your friends tell you it is safe to drive. What should you do?

Mark one answer
- **A.** Take their advice and drive
- ☑ **B.** Ignore your friends' advice and do not drive ✓
- **C.** Only drive if they come with you
- **D.** Drive for short distances only

296 You feel drowsy when driving. You should

Mark two answers
- ☑ **A.** Stop and rest as soon as possible ✓
- **B.** Turn the heater up to keep you warm and comfortable
- ☑ **C.** Make sure you have a good supply of fresh air ✓
- **D.** Continue with your journey but drive more slowly
- **E.** Close the car windows to help you concentrate

297 You are driving along a motorway and become tired. You should

Mark two answers

- ☑ **A.** Stop at the next service area and rest ✓
- ☑ **B.** Leave the motorway at the next exit and rest ✓
- ☐ **C.** Increase your speed and turn up the radio volume
- ☐ **D.** Close all your windows and set heating to warm
- ☐ **E.** Pull up on the hard shoulder and change drivers

298 You are taking drugs that are likely to affect your driving. What should you do?

Mark one answer

- ☑ **A.** Seek medical advice before driving ✓
- ☐ **B.** Limit your driving to essential journeys
- ☐ **C.** Only drive if accompanied by a full licence-holder
- ☐ **D.** Drive only for short distances

299 You are about to drive home. You feel very tired and have a severe headache. You should

Mark one answer

- ☑ **A.** Wait until you are fit and well before driving ✓
- ☐ **B.** Drive home but take a tablet for headaches
- ☐ **C.** Drive home if you can stay awake for the journey
- ☐ **D.** Wait for a short time then drive home slowly

300 If you are feeling tired it is best to stop as soon as you can. Until then you should

Mark one answer

- ☐ **A.** Increase your speed to find a stopping place quickly
- ☑ **B.** Ensure a supply of fresh air ✓
- ☐ **C.** Gently tap the steering wheel
- ☐ **D.** Keep changing speed to improve concentration

301 Your reactions will be much slower when driving

Mark one answer

- ☑ **A.** If tired ✓
- ☐ **B.** In fog
- ☐ **C.** Too quickly
- ☐ **D.** In rain

302 You are driving on a motorway. You feel tired. You should

Mark one answer

- ☐ **A.** Carry on but drive slowly
- ☑ **B.** Leave the motorway at the next exit ✓
- ☐ **C.** Complete your journey as quickly as possible
- ☐ **D.** Stop on the hard shoulder

303 If your motorway journey seems boring and you feel drowsy whilst driving you should

Mark one answer
- ☑ **A.** Open a window and drive to the next service area ✓
- ☐ **B.** Stop on the hard shoulder for a sleep
- ☐ **C.** Speed up to arrive at your destination sooner
- ☐ **D.** Slow down and let other drivers overtake

304 You are planning a long journey. It should take about six hours. Do you need to plan rest stops?

Mark one answer
- ☐ **A.** Yes, you should plan to stop after about four hours' driving
- ☑ **B.** Yes, regular stops help concentration ✓
- ☐ **C.** No, you will be less tired if you get there as soon as possible
- ☐ **D.** No, only fuel stops will be needed

305 Driving long distances can be tiring. You can prevent this by

Mark three answers
- ☑ **A.** Stopping every so often for a walk ✓
- ☑ **B.** Opening a window for some fresh air ✓
- ☑ **C.** Ensuring plenty of refreshment breaks ✓
- ☐ **D.** Completing the journey without stopping
- ☐ **E.** Eating a large meal before driving

306 To help concentration on long journeys you should stop frequently and

Mark one answer
- ☑ **A.** Have a rest ✓
- ☐ **B.** Fill up with fuel
- ☐ **C.** Eat a meal
- ☐ **D.** Take a shower

307 Which TWO things would help to keep you alert during a long journey?

Mark two answers
- ☐ **A.** Finishing your journey as fast as you can
- ☐ **B.** Keeping off the motorways and using country roads
- ☑ **C.** Making sure that you get plenty of fresh air ✓
- ☑ **D.** Making regular stops for refreshments ✓

308 Which THREE are likely to make you lose concentration while driving?

Mark three answers
- ☑ **A.** Looking at road maps ✓
- ☑ **B.** Listening to loud music ✓
- ☐ **C.** Using your windscreen washers
- ☐ **D.** Looking in your wing mirror
- ☑ **E.** Using a mobile phone ✓

309 A correct seating position will enable you to

Mark three answers
- [ ] **A.** Rest your head against the head restraint
- [x] **B.** Comfortably reach the pedals ✓
- [x] **C.** Have good visibility through the windows ✓
- [ ] **D.** Talk to all your passengers
- [x] **E.** Have a suitable grip on the steering wheel ✓
- [ ] **F.** Rest your hand on the gear lever

310 A driver pulls out of a side road in front of you. You have to brake hard. You should

Mark one answer
- [x] **A.** Ignore the error and stay calm ✓
- [ ] **B.** Flash your lights to show your annoyance
- [ ] **C.** Sound your horn to show your annoyance
- [ ] **D.** Overtake as soon as possible

311 A car driver pulls out causing you to brake. You should

Mark one answer
- [x] **A.** Keep calm and not retaliate ✓
- [ ] **B.** Overtake and sound your horn
- [ ] **C.** Drive close behind and sound your horn
- [ ] **D.** Flag the driver down and explain the mistake

312 Another driver does something that upsets you. You should

Mark one answer
- [x] **A.** Try not to react ✓
- [ ] **B.** Let them know how you feel
- [ ] **C.** Flash your headlamps several times
- [ ] **D.** Sound your horn

313 Another driver's behaviour has upset you. It may help if you

Mark one answer
- [x] **A.** Stop and take a break ✓
- [ ] **B.** Shout abusive language
- [ ] **C.** Gesture to them with your hand
- [ ] **D.** Follow their car, flashing the headlights

314 An elderly person's driving ability could be affected because they may be unable to

Mark one answer
- [ ] **A.** Obtain car insurance
- [ ] **B.** Understand road signs
- [x] **C.** React very quickly ✓
- [ ] **D.** Give signals correctly

315 You take the wrong route and find you are on a one-way street. You should

Mark one answer
- [ ] **A.** Reverse out of the road
- [ ] **B.** Turn round in a side road
- [x] **C.** Continue to the end of the road ✓
- [ ] **D.** Reverse into a driveway

316 You are driving on a country road. What should you expect to see coming towards you on YOUR side of the road?

Mark one answer
- [ ] **A.** Motorcycles
- [ ] **B.** Bicycles
- [✓] **C.** Pedestrians ✓
- [ ] **D.** Horse riders

317 Which sign means that there may be people walking along the road?

Mark one answer

A.

B.

C.
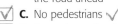

D. ✓
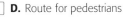

318 What does this sign mean?

Mark one answer
- [ ] **A.** Pedestrian crossing
- [ ] **B.** Pedestrians in the road ahead
- [✓] **C.** No pedestrians ✓
- [ ] **D.** Route for pedestrians

319 You are turning left into a side road. Pedestrians are crossing the road near the junction. You must

Mark one answer
- [ ] **A.** Wave them on
- [ ] **B.** Sound your horn
- [ ] **C.** Switch on your hazard lights
- [✓] **D.** Wait for them to cross ✓

320 You are turning left at a junction. Pedestrians have started to cross the road. You should

Mark one answer
- [ ] **A.** Go on, giving them plenty of room
- [ ] **B.** Stop and wave at them to cross
- [ ] **C.** Blow your horn and proceed
- [✓] **D.** Give way to them ✓

321 You are turning left from a main road into a side road. People are already crossing the road into which you are turning. You should

Mark one answer
- **A.** Continue, as it is your right of way
- **B.** Signal to them to continue crossing
- ☑ **C.** Wait and allow them to cross ✔
- **D.** Sound your horn to warn them of your presence

322 You are at a road junction, turning into a minor road. There are pedestrians crossing the minor road. You should

Mark one answer
- **A.** Stop and wave the pedestrians across
- **B.** Sound your horn to let the pedestrians know that you are there
- ☑ **C.** Give way to the pedestrians who are already crossing ✔
- **D.** Carry on; the pedestrians should give way to you

323 You are turning left into a side road. What hazards should you be especially aware of?

Mark one answer
- **A.** One-way street
- ☑ **B.** Pedestrians
- **C.** Traffic congestion
- **D.** Parked vehicles

324 You want to reverse into a side road. You are not sure that the area behind your car is clear. What should you do?

Mark one answer
- **A.** Look through the rear window only
- ☑ **B.** Get out and check ✔
- **C.** Check the mirrors only
- **D.** Carry on, assuming it is clear

325 You are about to reverse into a side road. A pedestrian wishes to cross behind you. You should

Mark one answer
- **A.** Wave to the pedestrian to stop
- ☑ **B.** Give way to the pedestrian ✔
- **C.** Wave to the pedestrian to cross
- **D.** Reverse before the pedestrian starts to cross

326 Who is especially in danger of not being seen as you reverse your car?

Mark one answer
- **A.** Motorcyclists
- **B.** Car drivers
- **C.** Cyclist
- ☑ **D.** Children ✔

327 You are reversing around a corner when you notice a pedestrian walking behind you. What should you do?

Mark one answer

- **A.** Slow down and wave the pedestrian across
- **B.** Continue reversing and steer round the pedestrian
- ☑ **C.** Stop and give way ✓
- **D.** Continue reversing and sound your horn

328 You intend to turn right into a side road. Just before turning you should check for motorcyclists who might be

Mark one answer

- **A.** Overtaking on your left
- **B.** Following you closely
- **C.** Emerging from the side road
- ☑ **D.** Overtaking on your right ✓

329 You want to turn right from a junction but your view is restricted by parked vehicles. What should you do?

Mark one answer

- **A.** Move out quickly, but be prepared to stop
- **B.** Sound your horn and pull out if there is no reply
- ☑ **C.** Stop, then move slowly forward until you have a clear view ✓
- **D.** Stop, get out and look along the main road to check

330 You are at the front of a queue of traffic waiting to turn right into a side road. Why is it important to check your right mirror just before turning?

Mark one answer

- **A.** To look for pedestrians about to cross
- ☑ **B.** To check for overtaking vehicles ✓
- **C.** To make sure the side road is clear
- **D.** To check for emerging traffic

331 In which THREE places would parking your vehicle cause danger or obstruction to other road users?

Mark three answers

- ☑ **A.** In front of a property entrance ✓
- ☑ **B.** At or near a bus stop ✓
- **C.** On your driveway
- **D.** In a marked parking space
- ☑ **E.** On the approach to a level crossing ✓

332 In which three places would parking cause an obstruction to others ?

Mark three answers

- ☑ **A.** Near the brow of a hill ✓
- **B.** In a lay-by
- **C.** Where the kerb is raised
- ☑ **D.** Where the kerb has been lowered for wheelchairs ✓
- ☑ **E.** At or near a bus stop ✓

333 What must a driver do at a pelican crossing when the amber light is flashing?

Mark one answer
- [ ] **A.** Signal the pedestrian to cross
- [ ] **B.** Always wait for the green light before proceeding
- [x] **C.** Give way to any pedestrians on the crossing ✓
- [ ] **D.** Wait for the red-and-amber light before proceeding

334 You have stopped at a pelican crossing. A disabled person is crossing slowly in front of you. The lights have now changed to green. You should

Mark two answers
- [x] **A.** Allow the person to cross ✓
- [ ] **B.** Drive in front of the person
- [ ] **C.** Drive behind the person
- [ ] **D.** Sound your horn
- [x] **E.** Be patient ✓
- [ ] **F.** Edge forward slowly

335 As you approach a pelican crossing the lights change to green. Elderly people are halfway across. You should

Mark one answer
- [ ] **A.** Wave them to cross as quickly as they can
- [ ] **B.** Rev your engine to make them hurry
- [ ] **C.** Flash your lights in case they have not heard you
- [x] **D.** Wait because they will take longer to cross ✓

336 A toucan crossing is different from other crossings because

Mark one answer
- [ ] **A.** Moped riders can use it
- [ ] **B.** It is controlled by a traffic warden
- [ ] **C.** It is controlled by two flashing lights
- [x] **D.** Cyclists can use it ✓

337 At toucan crossings

Mark two answers
- [x] **A.** There is no flashing amber light ✓
- [ ] **B.** Cyclists are not permitted
- [ ] **C.** There is a continuously flashing amber beacon
- [x] **D.** Pedestrians and cyclists may cross ✓
- [ ] **E.** You only stop if someone is waiting to cross

338 Look at this picture. What is the danger you should be most aware of?

Mark one answer
- [ ] **A.** The ice cream van may move off
- [ ] **B.** The driver of the ice cream van may get out
- [ ] **C.** The car on the left may move off
- [x] **D.** The child may run out into the road ✓

339 You are driving past parked cars. You notice a wheel of a bicycle sticking out between them. What should you do?

Mark one answer

- [ ] **A.** Accelerate past quickly and sound your horn
- [ ] **B.** Slow down and wave the cyclist across
- [ ] **C.** Brake sharply and flash your headlights
- [✓] **D.** Slow down and be prepared to stop for a cyclist ✓

340 You are driving past a line of parked cars. You notice a ball bouncing out into the road ahead. What should you do?

Mark one answer

- [ ] **A.** Continue driving at the same speed and sound your horn
- [ ] **B.** Continue driving at the same speed and flash your headlights
- [✓] **C.** Slow down and be prepared to stop for children ✓
- [ ] **D.** Stop and wave the children across to fetch their ball

341 What does this sign tell you?

Mark one answer

- [ ] **A.** No cycling
- [✓] **B.** Cycle route ahead ✓
- [ ] **C.** Route for cycles only
- [ ] **D.** End of cycle route

342 How will a school crossing patrol signal you to stop?

Mark one answer

- [ ] **A.** By pointing to children on the opposite pavement
- [ ] **B.** By displaying a red light
- [✓] **C.** By displaying a stop sign ✓
- [ ] **D.** By giving you an arm signal

343 You are approaching a school crossing patrol. When this sign is held up you must

Mark one answer

- [✓] **A.** Stop and allow any children to cross ✓
- [ ] **B.** Stop and beckon the children to cross
- [ ] **C.** Stop only if the children are on a pedestrian crossing
- [ ] **D.** Stop only when the children are actually crossing the road

344 Where would you see this sign?

Mark one answer

A. In the window of a car taking children to school

B. At the side of the road

C. At playground areas

☑ D. On the rear of a school bus or coach ✓

345 Where would you see this sign?

Mark one answer

A. On the approach to a school crossing

B. At a playground entrance

☑ C. On a school bus ✓

D. At a 'pedestrians only' area

346 You are parking your vehicle in the street. The car parked in front of you is displaying an orange badge. You should

Mark one answer

A. Park close to it to save road space

☑ B. Allow room for a wheelchair ✓

C. Wait until the orange-badge holder returns

D. Park with two wheels on the pavement

347 You are following a car driven by an elderly driver. You should

Mark one answer

A. Expect the driver to drive badly

B. Flash your lights and overtake

☑ C. Be aware that the driver's reactions may not be as fast as yours ✓

D. Stay close behind and drive carefully

348 Which sign tells you that pedestrians may be walking in the road as there is no pavement?

Mark one answer

☑ A. ✓   B.

C.   D.

349 Which sign means there may be elderly pedestrians likely to cross the road ?

Mark one answer

☑ A. ✓   B.

C.   D.

350 What does this sign mean?

Mark one answer

- [ ] **A.** No route for pedestrians and cyclists
- [ ] **B.** A route for pedestrians only
- [ ] **C.** A route for cyclists only
- [✓] **D.** A route for pedestrians and cyclists ✓

351 You see a pedestrian carrying a <u>white</u> stick. This shows that the person is

→ слепой - белая трость

Mark one answer

- [ ] **A.** Disabled
- [ ] **B.** Deaf
- [ ] **C.** Elderly
- [✓] **D.** Blind —

352 You see a pedestrian with a <u>white</u> stick and red band. This means that the person is

глухой
слепой

Mark one answer

- [ ] **A.** Physically disabled
- [ ] **B.** Deaf only
- [ ] **C.** Blind only
- [✓] **D.** Deaf and blind ✓

353 You are driving towards a zebra crossing. Waiting to cross is a person in a wheelchair. You should

Mark one answer

- [ ] **A.** Continue on your way
- [ ] **B.** Wave to the person to cross
- [ ] **C.** Wave to the person to wait
- [✓] **D.** Be prepared to stop ✓

354 What action would you take when elderly people are crossing the road?

Mark one answer

- [ ] **A.** Wave them across so they know that you have seen them
- [✓] **B.** Be patient and allow them to cross in their own time ✓
- [ ] **C.** Rev the engine to let them know that you are waiting
- [ ] **D.** Tap the horn in case they are hard of hearing

355 You see two elderly pedestrians about to cross the road ahead. You should

Mark one answer

- [ ] **A.** Expect them to wait for you to pass
- [ ] **B.** Speed up to get past them quickly
- [ ] **C.** Stop and wave them across the road
- [✓] **D.** Be careful, they may misjudge your speed ✓

356 You are following a motorcyclist on an <u>uneven</u> road. You should

Mark one answer

- [ ] **A.** Allow less room to ensure that you can be seen in their mirrors
- [ ] **B.** Overtake immediately
- [✓] **C.** Allow extra room in case they swerve to avoid pot-holes ✓ ямы на дороге
- [ ] **D.** Allow the same room as normal because motorcyclists are not affected by road surfaces

357 What does this sign mean?

Mark one answer
- **A.** Contra-flow pedal cycle lane
- ✓ **B.** With-flow pedal cycle lane ✓
- **C.** Pedal cycles and buses only
- **D.** No pedal cycles or buses

358 You should NEVER attempt to overtake a cyclist

Mark one answer
- ✓ **A.** Just before you turn left ✓
- **B.** Just before you turn right
- **C.** On a one-way street
- **D.** On a dual carriageway

359 You are driving behind a cyclist. You wish to turn left just ahead. You should

Mark one answer
- **A.** Overtake the cyclist before the junction
- **B.** Pull alongside the cyclist and stay level until after the junction
- ✓ **C.** Hold back until the cyclist has passed the junction ✓
- **D.** Go around the cyclist on the junction

360 You are coming up to a roundabout. A cyclist is signalling to turn right. What should you do?

Mark one answer
- **A.** Overtake on the right
- **B.** Give a horn warning
- **C.** Signal the cyclist to move across
- ✓ **D.** Give the cyclist plenty of room ✓

361 You are driving behind two cyclists. They approach a roundabout in the left-hand lane. In which direction should you expect the cyclists to go?

Mark one answer
- **A.** Left
- **B.** Right
- ✓ **C.** Any direction ✓
- **D.** Straight ahead

362 You are approaching this roundabout and see the cyclist signal right. Why is the cyclist keeping to the left?

Mark one answer
- **A.** It is a quicker route for the cyclist
- **B.** The cyclist is going to turn left instead
- **C.** The cyclist thinks the Highway Code does not apply to bicycles
- ✓ **D.** The cyclist is slower and more vulnerable ✓

363 When you are overtaking a cyclist you should leave as much room as you would give to a car. What is the main reason for this?

Mark one answer
- **A.** The cyclist might change lanes
- **B.** The cyclist might get off the bike
- ✓ **C.** The cyclist might swerve ✓
- **D.** The cyclist might have to make a right turn

364 Which TWO should you allow extra room when overtaking?

Mark two answers
- ✓ **A.** Motorcycles ✓
- **B.** Tractors
- ✓ **C.** Bicycles ✓
- **D.** Road-sweeping vehicles *- xxx xxx*

365 Why should you allow extra room when overtaking a motorcyclist on a windy day?

Mark one answer
- **A.** The rider may turn off suddenly to get out of the wind
- ✓ **B.** The rider may be blown across in front of you ✓
- **C.** The rider may stop suddenly
- **D.** The rider may be travelling faster than normal

366 Which type of vehicle is most affected by strong winds?

Mark one answer
- **A.** Tractor
- ✓ **B.** Motorcycle ✓
- **C.** Car
- **D.** Tanker

367 Why should you look particularly for motorcyclists and cyclists at junctions?

Mark one answer
- **A.** They may want to turn into the side road
- **B.** They may slow down to let you turn
- ✓ **C.** They are harder to see ✓
- **D.** They might not see you turn

368 You are waiting to come out of a side road. Why should you watch carefully for motorcycles?

Mark one answer
- **A.** Motorcycles are usually faster than cars
- **B.** Police patrols often use motorcycles
- ✓ **C.** Motorcycles are small and hard to see ✓
- **D.** Motorcycles have right of way

369 Where should you take particular care to look out for motorcyclists and cyclists?

Mark one answer
- **A.** On dual carriageways
- ✓ **B.** At junctions ✓
- **C.** At zebra crossings
- **D.** On one-way streets

370 In daylight, an approaching motorcyclist is using a dipped headlight. Why?

Mark one answer
- ☑ **A.** So that the rider can be seen more easily ✓
- ☐ **B.** To stop the battery over-charging
- ☐ **C.** To improve the rider's vision
- ☐ **D.** The rider is inviting you to proceed

371 Where in particular should you look out for motorcyclists?

Mark one answer
- ☐ **A.** In a filling station
- ☑ **B.** At a road junction ✓
- ☐ **C.** Near a service area
- ☐ **D.** When entering a car park

372 Motorcycle riders are vulnerable because they

Mark one answer
- ☐ **A.** Are easy for other road users to see
- ☑ **B.** Are difficult for other road users to see ✓
- ☐ **C.** Are likely to have breakdowns
- ☐ **D.** Cannot give arm signals

373 Motorcyclists should wear bright clothing mainly because

Mark one answer
- ☐ **A.** They must do so by law
- ☐ **B.** It helps keep them cool in summer
- ☐ **C.** The colours are popular
- ☑ **D.** Drivers often do not see them ✓

374 Motorcyclists ride in daylight with their headlights switched on because

Mark one answer
- ☐ **A.** It is a legal requirement
- ☐ **B.** There is a speed trap ahead
- ☑ **C.** They need to be seen ✓
- ☐ **D.** There are speed humps ahead

375 There is a slow-moving motorcyclist ahead of you. You are unsure what the rider is going to do. You should

Mark one answer
- ☐ **A.** Pass on the left
- ☐ **B.** Pass on the right
- ☑ **C.** Stay behind ✓
- ☐ **D.** Move closer

376 You are driving behind a moped. You want to turn left just ahead. You should

Mark one answer
- ☐ **A.** Overtake the moped before the junction
- ☐ **B.** Pull alongside the moped and stay level until just before the junction
- ☐ **C.** Sound your horn as a warning and pull in front of the moped
- ☑ **D.** Stay behind until the moped has passed the junction ✓

377 Motorcyclists will often look round over their right shoulder just before turning right. This is because

Mark one answer
- [ ] **A.** They need to listen for following traffic
- [ ] **B.** Motorcycles do not have mirrors
- [ ] **C.** Looking around helps them balance as they turn
- [x] **D.** They need to check for traffic in their blind area ✓

378 At road junctions which of the following are most vulnerable?

Mark three answers
- [x] **A.** Cyclists ✓
- [x] **B.** Motorcyclists ✓
- [x] **C.** Pedestrians ✓
- [ ] **D.** Car drivers
- [ ] **E.** Lorry drivers

379 When emerging from a side road into a queue of traffic, which vehicles can be especially difficult to see?

Mark one answer
- [x] **A.** Motorcycles ✓
- [ ] **B.** Tractors
- [ ] **C.** Milk floats
- [ ] **D.** Cars

380 You want to turn right from a main road into a side road. Just before turning you should

Mark one answer
- [ ] **A.** Cancel your right-turn signal
- [ ] **B.** Select first gear
- [x] **C.** Check for traffic overtaking on your right ✓
- [ ] **D.** Stop and set the handbrake

381 Motorcyclists are particularly vulnerable

Mark one answer
- [ ] **A.** When moving off
- [ ] **B.** On dual carriageways
- [x] **C.** When approaching junctions ✓
- [ ] **D.** On motorways

382 Which of the following are hazards motorcyclists present in queues of traffic?

Mark three answers
- [x] **A.** Cutting in just in front of you ✓
- [ ] **B.** Riding in single file
- [x] **C.** Passing very close to your car ✓
- [ ] **D.** Riding with their headlamp on dipped beam
- [x] **E.** Filtering between the lanes ✓

383 You are driving on a main road. You intend to turn right into a side road. Just before turning you should

Mark one answer
- [ ] **A.** Adjust your interior mirror
- [ ] **B.** Flash your headlamps
- [ ] **C.** Steer over to the left
- [x] **D.** Check for traffic overtaking on your offside ✓

384 When driving, ahead of you there is a vehicle with a flashing amber beacon. This means it is

Mark one answer
- ☑ **A.** Slow-moving ✓
- ☐ **B.** Broken down
- ☐ **C.** A doctor's car
- ☐ **D.** A school crossing patrol

385 You are driving in slow-moving queues of traffic. Just before changing lane you should

Mark one answer
- ☐ **A.** Sound the horn
- ☑ **B.** Look for motorcyclists filtering through the traffic ✓
- ☐ **C.** Give a 'slowing down' arm signal
- ☐ **D.** Change down to first gear

386 An injured motorcyclist is lying unconscious in the road. You should

Mark one answer
- ☐ **A.** Remove the safety helmet
- ☑ **B.** Seek medical assistance ✓
- ☐ **C.** Move the person off the road
- ☐ **D.** Remove the leather jacket

387 You are driving in town. There is a bus at the bus stop on the other side of the road. Why should you be careful?

Mark one answer
- ☐ **A.** The bus may have broken down
- ☑ **B.** Pedestrians may come from behind the bus ✓
- ☐ **C.** The bus may move off suddenly
- ☐ **D.** The bus may remain stationary

388 How should you overtake horse riders?

Mark one answer
- ☐ **A.** Drive up close and overtake as soon as possible
- ☐ **B.** Speed is not important but allow plenty of room
- ☐ **C.** Use your horn just once to warn them
- ☑ **D.** Drive slowly and leave plenty of room ✓

389 You notice horse riders in front. What should you do FIRST?

Mark one answer
- ☐ **A.** Pull out to the middle of the road
- ☑ **B.** Be prepared to slow down ✓
- ☐ **C.** Accelerate around them
- ☐ **D.** Signal right

390 You are driving on a narrow country road. Where would you find it most difficult to see horses and riders ahead of you?

Mark one answer
- [x] **A.** On left-hand bends ✓
- [ ] **B.** When travelling downhill
- [ ] **C.** When travelling uphill
- [ ] **D.** On right-hand bends

391 A horse rider is in the left-hand lane approaching a roundabout. The driver behind should expect the rider to

Mark one answer
- [x] **A.** Go in any direction ✓
- [ ] **B.** Turn right
- [ ] **C.** Turn left
- [ ] **D.** Go ahead

392 You are approaching a roundabout. There are horses just ahead of you. You should

Mark two answers
- [x] **A.** Be prepared to stop ✓
- [ ] **B.** Treat them like any other vehicle
- [x] **C.** Give them plenty of room ✓
- [ ] **D.** Accelerate past as quickly as possible
- [ ] **E.** Sound your horn as a warning

393 You see some horse riders as you approach a roundabout. They are signalling right but keeping well to the left. You should

Mark one answer
- [ ] **A.** Proceed as normal
- [ ] **B.** Keep close to them
- [ ] **C.** Cut in front of them
- [x] **D.** Stay well back ✓

394 Which THREE should you do when passing sheep on a road?

Mark three answers
- [x] **A.** Allow plenty of room ✓
- [x] **B.** Drive very slowly ✓
- [ ] **C.** Pass quickly but quietly
- [x] **D.** Be ready to stop ✓
- [ ] **E.** Briefly sound your horn

395 What is the most common factor in causing road accidents?

Mark one answer
- [ ] **A.** Weather conditions
- [x] **B.** Driver error ✓
- [ ] **C.** Road conditions
- [ ] **D.** Mechanical failure

396 You have a collision whilst your car is moving. What is the first thing you must do?

Mark one answer
- **A.** Stop only if there are injured people
- **B.** Call the emergency services
- ☑ **C.** Stop at the scene of the accident ✓
- **D.** Call your insurance company

397 How would you react to other drivers who appear to be inexperienced?

Mark one answer
- **A.** Sound your horn to warn them of your presence
- ☑ **B.** Be patient and prepared for them to react more slowly ✓
- **C.** Flash your headlights to indicate that it is safe for them to proceed
- **D.** Overtake them as soon as possible

398 As a new driver, how can you decrease your risk of accidents on the motorway?

Mark one answer
- **A.** By keeping up with the car in front
- **B.** By never driving over 45mph
- **C.** By driving only in the nearside lane
- ☑ **D.** By taking further training ✓

399 Which age group is most likely to be involved in a road accident?

Mark one answer
- **A.** 36 to 45-year-olds
- **B.** 55-year-olds and over
- **C.** 46 to 55-year-olds
- ☑ **D.** 17 to 25-year-olds ✓

400 You are following a learner driver who stalls at a junction. You should

Mark one answer
- ☑ **A.** Be patient as you expect them to make mistakes ✓
- **B.** Drive up close behind and flash your headlamps
- **C.** Start to rev your engine if they take too long to re-start
- **D.** Immediately steer around them and drive on

401 A friend wants to teach you to drive a car. They must

Mark one answer
- **A.** Be over 21 and have held a full licence for at least two years
- **B.** Be over 18 and hold an advanced driver's certificate
- **C.** Be over 18 and have fully comprehensive insurance
- ☑ **D.** Be over 21 and have held a full licence for at least three years ✓

402 Your vehicle hits a pedestrian at 40mph. The pedestrian will

Mark one answer

- [ ] **A.** Certainly be killed ✓
- [ ] **B.** Certainly survive
- [✓] **C.** Probably be killed _верно._
- [ ] **D.** Probably survive

403 At night you see a pedestrian wearing reflective clothing and carrying a bright red light. What does this mean?

Mark one answer

- [ ] **A.** You are approaching roadworks
- [✓] **B.** You are approaching an organised walk
- [ ] **C.** You are approaching a slow-moving vehicle
- [ ] **D.** You are approaching an accident black spot

404 You are dazzled at night by a vehicle behind you. You should

Mark one answer

- [✓] **A.** Set your mirror to anti-dazzle ✓
- [ ] **B.** Set your mirror to dazzle the other driver
- [ ] **C.** Brake sharply to a stop
- [ ] **D.** Switch your rear lights on and off

405 The road is wet. Why might a motorcyclist steer round drain covers on a bend?

Mark one answer

- **A.** To avoid puncturing the tyres on the edge of the drain covers
- ✓ **B.** To prevent the motorcycle sliding on the metal drain covers
- **C.** To help judge the bend using the drain covers as marker points
- **D.** To avoid splashing pedestrians on the pavement

406 It is very windy. You are behind a motorcyclist who is overtaking a high-sided vehicle. What should you do?

Mark one answer

- **A.** Overtake the motorcyclist immediately
- ✓ **B.** Keep well back
- **C.** Stay level with the motorcyclist
- **D.** Keep close to the motorcyclist

407 It is very windy. You are about to overtake a motorcyclist. You should

Mark one answer

- **A.** Overtake slowly
- ✓ **B.** Allow extra room
- **C.** Sound your horn
- **D.** Keep close as you pass

408 You are about to overtake a slow-moving motorcyclist. Which one of these signs would make you take special care?

Mark one answer

✓ **A.** ☐ **B.** ☐ **C.** ☐ **D.**

409 You are waiting to emerge left from a minor road. A large vehicle is approaching from the right. You have time to turn, but you should wait. Why?

Mark one answer

- ✓ **A.** The large vehicle can easily hide an overtaking vehicle
- **B.** The large vehicle can turn suddenly
- **C.** The large vehicle is difficult to steer in a straight line
- **D.** The large vehicle can easily hide vehicles from the left

410 You are following a large articulated vehicle. It is going to turn left into a narrow road. What action should you take?

Mark one answer

- **A.** Move out and overtake on the offside
- **B.** Pass on the left as the vehicle moves out
- ✓ **C.** Be prepared to stop behind
- **D.** Overtake quickly before the lorry moves out

411 You are following a long vehicle. It approaches a crossroads and signals left, but moves out to the right. You should

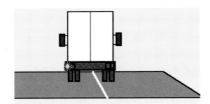

Mark one answer
- [ ] **A.** Get closer in order to pass it quickly
- [✓] **B.** Stay well back and give it room ✓
- [ ] **C.** Assume the signal is wrong and it is really turning right
- [ ] **D.** Overtake as it starts to slow down

412 You are following a long vehicle approaching a crossroads. The driver signals right but moves close to the left-hand kerb. What should you do?

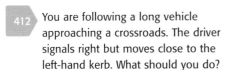

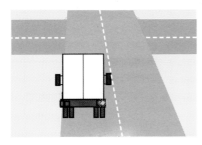

Mark one answer
- [ ] **A.** Warn the driver of the wrong signal
- [✓] **B.** Wait behind the long vehicle ✓
- [ ] **C.** Report the driver to the police
- [ ] **D.** Overtake on the right-hand side

413 You are approaching a mini-roundabout. The long vehicle in front is signalling left but positioned over to the right. You should

Mark one answer
- [ ] **A.** Sound your horn
- [ ] **B.** Overtake on the left
- [ ] **C.** Follow the same course as the lorry
- [✓] **D.** Keep well back ✓

414 You are following a large vehicle. Side and end markers are being displayed. This means the load

Mark one answer
- [ ] **A.** Is higher than normal
- [ ] **B.** May be flammable
- [ ] **C.** Is in two parts
- [✓] **D.** Overhangs at the rear ✓

415 You are towing a caravan. Which is the safest type of rear view mirror to use?

Mark one answer
- [ ] **A.** Interior wide-angle-view mirror
- [✓] **B.** Extended-arm side mirrors ✓
- [ ] **C.** Ordinary door mirrors
- [ ] **D.** Ordinary interior mirror

416 You keep well back while waiting to overtake a large vehicle. Another car fills the gap. You should

Mark one answer

- **A.** Sound your horn
- ✓ **B.** Drop back further —
- **C.** Flash your headlights
- **D.** Start to overtake

417 Before overtaking a large vehicle you should keep well back. Why is this?

Mark one answer

- **A.** To give acceleration space to overtake quickly on blind bends
- ✓ **B.** To get the best view of the road ahead ✓
- **C.** To leave a gap in case the vehicle stops and rolls back
- **D.** To offer other drivers a safe gap if they want to overtake you

418 You wish to overtake a long, slow-moving vehicle on a busy road. You should

Mark one answer

- **A.** Follow it closely and keep moving out to see the road ahead *а е 9н сделанр дан*
- **B.** Flash your headlights for the oncoming traffic to give way
- **C.** Stay behind until the driver waves you past
- ✓ **D.** Keep well back until you can see that it is clear ✓

419 You are driving downhill. There is a car parked on the other side of the road. Large, slow lorries are coming towards you. You should

Mark one answer

- **A.** Keep going because you have the right of way
- ✓ **B.** Slow down and give way ✓
- **C.** Speed up and get past quickly
- **D.** Pull over on the right behind the parked car *Иначе большие машины*

420 When about to overtake a long vehicle you should

Mark one answer

- **A.** Sound the horn to warn the driver that you're there
- ✓ **B.** Stay well back from the lorry to obtain a better view ✓
- **C.** Drive close to the lorry in order to pass more quickly
- **D.** Flash your lights and wait for the driver to signal when it is safe

421 Why is passing a lorry more risky than passing a car?

Mark one answer

- ✓ **A.** Lorries are longer than cars ✓
- **B.** Lorries may suddenly pull up
- **C.** The brakes of lorries are not as good
- **D.** Lorries climb hills more slowly

422 As a driver, why should you be more careful where trams operate?

Mark two answers

- **A.** Because they do not have a horn
- **C.** Because they are silent ✓
- **B.** Because they do not stop for cars
- **D.** Because they cannot steer to avoid you ✓
- **E.** Because they do not have lights

423 You are driving along a road and you see this signal. It means

Mark one answer

- **A.** Cars must stop
- **B.** Trams must stop ✓
- **C.** Both trams and cars must stop
- **D.** Both trams and cars can continue

424 You are travelling behind a bus that pulls up at a bus stop. What should you do?

Mark two answers

- **A.** Accelerate past the bus sounding your horn
- **B.** Watch carefully for pedestrians ✓
- **C.** Be ready to give way to the bus ✓
- **D.** Pull in closely behind the bus

425 You are driving in town. Ahead of you a bus is at a bus stop. Which two of the following should you do?

Mark two answers

- **A.** Be prepared to give way if the bus suddenly moves off ✓
- **B.** Continue at the same speed but sound your horn as a warning
- **C.** Watch carefully for the sudden appearance of pedestrians ✓
- **D.** Pass the bus as quickly as you possibly can

426 When you approach a bus signalling to move off from a bus stop you should

Mark one answer

- **A.** Get past before it moves
- **B.** Allow it to pull away, if it is safe to do so ✓
- **C.** Flash your headlights as you approach
- **D.** Signal left and wave the bus on

427 Which of these vehicles is LEAST likely to be affected by crosswinds?

Mark one answer

- **A.** Cyclists
- **B.** Motorcyclists
- **C.** High-sided vehicles
- **D.** Cars ✓

428 What does 'tailgating' mean?

Mark one answer

- [ ] **A.** When a vehicle delivering goods has its tailgate down
- [ ] **B.** When a vehicle is travelling with its back doors open
- [x] **C.** When a driver is following another vehicle too closely ✓
- [ ] **D.** When stationary vehicles are too close in a queue

429 You are following a large lorry on a wet road. Spray makes it difficult to see. You should

Mark one answer

- [x] **A.** Drop back until you can see better ✓
- [ ] **B.** Put your headlights on full beam
- [ ] **C.** Keep close to the lorry, away from the spray
- [ ] **D.** Speed up and overtake quickly

430 You are driving on a wet motorway with surface spray. You should use

Mark one answer

- [ ] **A.** Your hazard flashers
- [x] **B.** Dipped headlights
- [ ] **C.** Your rear fog lights
- [ ] **D.** Your sidelights

431 You are driving in heavy traffic on a wet road. Spray makes it difficult to be seen. You should use your

Mark two answers

- [ ] **A.** Full beam headlights
- [x] **B.** Rear fog lights if visibility is less than 100 metres (328 feet)
- [ ] **C.** Rear fog lights if visibility is more than 100 metres (328 feet)
- [x] **D.** Dipped headlights
- [ ] **E.** Side lights only

432 Some two-way roads are divided into three lanes. Why are these particularly dangerous?

Mark one answer

- [x] **A.** Traffic in both directions can use the middle lane to overtake ✓
- [ ] **B.** Traffic can travel faster in poor weather conditions
- [ ] **C.** Traffic can overtake on the left
- [ ] **D.** Traffic uses the middle lane for emergencies only

433 What are TWO main reasons why coasting downhill is wrong?

Mark two answers
- [ ] **A.** Fuel consumption will be higher
- [x] **B.** The vehicle will pick up speed ✓
- [ ] **C.** It puts more wear and tear on the tyres
- [x] **D.** You have less braking and steering control ✓
- [ ] **E.** It damages the engine

434 You should avoid 'coasting' your vehicle because it could

Mark one answer
- [ ] **A.** Damage the suspension
- [ ] **B.** Increase tyre wear
- [ ] **C.** Flatten the battery
- [x] **D.** Reduce steering control ✓

435 Why is coasting wrong?

Mark one answer
- [ ] **A.** It will cause the car to skid
- [ ] **B.** It will make the engine stall
- [ ] **C.** The engine will run faster
- [x] **D.** There is no engine braking ✓

436 Hills can affect the performance of your vehicle. Which TWO apply when driving up steep hills?

Mark two answers
- [ ] **A.** Higher gears will pull better ✓
- [x] **B.** You will slow down sooner
- [ ] **C.** Overtaking will be easier
- [x] **D.** The engine will work harder ✓
- [ ] **E.** The steering will feel heavier

437 You are approaching a bend at speed. You should begin to brake

Mark one answer
- [ ] **A.** On the bend
- [ ] **B.** After the bend
- [ ] **C.** After changing gear
- [x] **D.** Before the bend ✓

438 You are following a vehicle at a safe distance on a wet road. Another driver overtakes you and pulls into the gap you have left. What should you do?

Mark one answer
- [ ] **A.** Flash your headlights as a warning
- [ ] **B.** Try to overtake safely as soon as you can
- [x] **C.** Drop back to regain a safe distance ✓
- [ ] **D.** Stay close to the other vehicle until it moves on

439 You are driving in the left-hand lane of a dual carriageway. Another vehicle overtakes and pulls in front of you, leaving you without enough separation distance. You should

Mark one answer
- [ ] **A.** Move to the right-hand lane
- [ ] **B.** Continue as you are
- [x] **C.** Drop back ✓
- [ ] **D.** Sound your horn

440 In which THREE of these situations may you overtake another vehicle on the left?

Mark three answers

- ☑ **A.** When you are in a one-way street ✓
- ☐ **B.** When approaching a motorway slip road where you will be turning off
- ☑ **C.** When the vehicle in front is signalling to turn right ✓
- ☐ **D.** When a slower vehicle is travelling in the right-hand lane of a dual carriageway
- ☑ **E.** In slow-moving traffic queues when traffic in the right-hand lane is moving more slowly ✓

441 You are driving on the motorway in windy conditions. When passing high-sided vehicles you should

Mark one answer

- ☐ **A.** Increase your speed
- ☑ **B.** Be wary of a sudden gust ✓
- ☐ **C.** Drive alongside very closely
- ☐ **D.** Expect normal conditions

442 Which THREE of the following will affect your stopping distance?

Mark three answers

- ☑ **A.** How fast you are going ✓
- ☑ **B.** The tyres on your vehicle ✓
- ☐ **C.** The time of day
- ☑ **D.** The weather ✓
- ☐ **E.** The street lighting

443 You are travelling in very heavy rain. Your overall stopping distance is likely to be

Mark one answer

- ☑ **A.** Doubled ✓
- ☐ **B.** Halved
- ☐ **C.** Up to 10 times greater
- ☐ **D.** No different

444 Motorcyclists are more at risk from other road users because they

Mark one answer

- ☐ **A.** Are less experienced than other drivers
- ☐ **B.** Are more likely to break down than other motorists
- ☐ **C.** Are always faster than other drivers
- ☑ **D.** Are more difficult to see than other drivers ✓

445 To correct a rear-wheel skid you should

Mark one answer

- ☐ **A.** Not steer at all
- ☐ **B.** Steer away from it
- ☑ **C.** Steer into it ✓
- ☐ **D.** Apply your handbrake

446 When snow is falling heavily you should

Mark one answer

- ☐ **A.** Drive as long as your headlights are used
- ☐ **B.** Not drive unless you have a mobile phone
- ☐ **C.** Drive only when your journey is short
- ☑ **D.** Not drive unless it is essential ✓

А как же люди в России живут? Что, всю зиму дома сидеть?

447 You are driving on an icy road. What distance should you drive from the car in front?

Mark one answer
- **A.** Eight times the normal distance
- **B.** Six times the normal distance
- **C.** Ten times the normal distance ✓
- **D.** Four times the normal distance

448 You are driving in very wet weather. Your vehicle begins to slide. This effect is called

Mark one answer
- **A.** Hosing
- **B.** Weaving
- **C.** Aquaplaning ✓
- **D.** Fading

449 Why should you test your brakes after this hazard?

Ford

Mark one answer
- **A.** Because you will be driving on a slippery road
- **B.** Because your brakes will be soaking wet ✓
- **C.** Because you will have driven down a long hill
- **D.** Because you will have just crossed a long bridge

450 You have to make a journey in fog. What are the TWO most important things you should do before you set out?

Mark two answers
- **A.** Top up the radiator with antifreeze
- **B.** Make sure that you have a warning triangle in the vehicle
- **C.** Check that your lights are working ✓
- **D.** Check the battery
- **E.** Make sure that the windows are clean ✓

451 You have to make a journey in foggy conditions. You should

Mark one answer
- **A.** Follow closely other vehicles' tail lights
- **B.** Never use demisters and windscreen wipers
- **C.** Leave plenty of time for your journey ✓
- **D.** Keep two seconds behind other vehicles

452 Front fog lights may be used ONLY if

Mark one answer
- **A.** Visibility is seriously reduced ✓
- **B.** They are fitted above the bumper
- **C.** They are not as bright as the headlights
- **D.** An audible warning device is used

453 Front fog lights may be used ONLY

Mark one answer
- [ ] **A.** If they are not as bright as the headlights
- [x] **B.** When visibility is seriously reduced ✓
- [ ] **C.** Between dusk and dawn
- [ ] **D.** During 'lighting up' times only

Mark one answer
- [x] **A.** When visibility is less than 100 metres (328 feet) ✓
- [ ] **B.** At any time to be noticed
- [ ] **C.** Instead of headlights on high speed roads
- [ ] **D.** When dazzled by the lights of oncoming vehicles

---

454 Front fog lights may be used ONLY if

Mark one answer
- [ ] **A.** Your headlights are not working
- [ ] **B.** They are operated with rear fog lights
- [ ] **C.** They were fitted by the vehicle manufacturer
- [x] **D.** Visibility is seriously reduced ✓

457 Front fog lights should be used ONLY when

Mark one answer
- [ ] **A.** Travelling in very light rain
- [x] **B.** Visibility is seriously reduced ✓
- [ ] **C.** Daylight is fading
- [ ] **D.** Driving after midnight

---

455 Front fog lights may be used ONLY if

Mark one answer
- [ ] **A.** They prevent headlight glare on a wet road
- [ ] **B.** You wish to overtake in bad weather
- [x] **C.** Visibility is seriously reduced ✓
- [ ] **D.** Fitted by the manufacturer

458 Front fog lights should be used

Mark one answer
- [x] **A.** When visibility is reduced to 100 metres (328 feet) ✓
- [ ] **B.** As a warning to oncoming traffic
- [ ] **C.** When driving during the hours of darkness
- [ ] **D.** In any conditions and at any time

---

456 You may drive with front fog lights switched on

459 Using front fog lights in clear daylight will

Mark one answer
- [ ] **A.** Flatten the battery
- [x] **B.** Dazzle other drivers ✓
- [ ] **C.** Improve your visibility
- [ ] **D.** Increase your awareness

460 You may use front fog lights with headlights ONLY when visibility is reduced to less than

Mark one answer
- [x] **A.** 100 metres (328 feet) ✓
- [ ] **B.** 200 metres (656 feet)
- [ ] **C.** 300 metres (984 feet)
- [ ] **D.** 400 metres (1312 feet)

461 You are following other vehicles in fog with your lights on. How else can you reduce the chances of being involved in an accident?

Mark one answer
- [ ] **A.** Keep close to the vehicle in front
- [ ] **B.** Use your main beam instead of dipped headlights
- [ ] **C.** Keep together with the faster vehicles
- [x] **D.** Reduce your speed and increase the gap ✓

462 Why should you always reduce your speed when driving in fog?

Mark one answer
- [ ] **A.** Because the brakes do not work as well
- [ ] **B.** Because you could be dazzled by other people's fog lights
- [ ] **C.** Because the engine's colder
- [x] **D.** Because it is more difficult to see events ahead ✓

463 You are driving in fog. Why should you keep well back from the vehicle in front?

Mark one answer
- [ ] **A.** In case it changes direction suddenly
- [ ] **B.** In case its fog lights dazzle you
- [x] **C.** In case it stops suddenly ✓
- [ ] **D.** In case its brake lights dazzle you

464 You should switch your rear fog lights on when visibility drops below

Mark one answer
- [ ] **A.** Your overall stopping distance
- [ ] **B.** Ten car lengths
- [ ] **C.** 200 metres (656 feet)
- [x] **D.** 100 metres (328 feet) ✓

465 You should only use rear fog lights when you cannot see further than about

Mark one answer
- [x] **A.** 100 metres (328 feet) ✓
- [ ] **B.** 200 metres (656 feet)
- [ ] **C.** 250 metres (820 feet)
- [ ] **D.** 150 metres (492 feet)

466 You should use rear fog lights when

Mark one answer
- [ ] **A.** Vehicles are following too closely
- [x] **B.** Visibility is reduced to 100 metres (328 feet) ✓
- [ ] **C.** Very bright sunshine is dazzling motorists
- [ ] **D.** Driving in busy fast-moving traffic

467 Using rear fog lights in clear daylight will

Mark one answer

- [ ] **A.** Be useful when towing a trailer
- [ ] **B.** Give extra protection
- [x] **C.** Dazzle other drivers ✓
- [ ] **D.** Make following drivers keep back

468 You are driving on a clear dry night with your rear fog lights switched on. This may

Mark two answers **NI**

- [ ] **A.** Reduce glare from the road surface
- [x] **B.** Make other drivers think you are braking
- [ ] **C.** Give a better view of the road ahead
- [x] **D.** Dazzle following drivers ✓
- [ ] **E.** help your indicators to be seen more clearly

469 Why is it dangerous to leave rear fog lights on when they are not needed?

Mark two answers **NI**

- [x] **A.** Brake lights are less clear
- [x] **B.** Following drivers can be dazzled ✓
- [ ] **C.** Electrical systems could be overloaded
- [ ] **D.** Direction indicators may not work properly
- [ ] **E.** The battery could fail

470 Whilst driving, the fog clears and you can see more clearly. You must remember to

Mark one answer

- [x] **A.** Switch off the fog lights ✓
- [ ] **B.** Reduce your speed
- [ ] **C.** Switch off the demister
- [ ] **D.** Close any open windows

471 You are driving in thick fog using fog lights. When visibility improves you MUST

Mark one answer

- [ ] **A.** Maintain your speed
- [ ] **B.** Keep them on
- [ ] **C.** Increase your speed
- [x] **D.** Switch them off ✓

472 You have just driven out of fog. Visibility is now good. You MUST

Mark one answer

- [x] **A.** Switch off all your fog lights ✓
- [ ] **B.** Keep your rear fog lights on
- [ ] **C.** Keep your front fog lights on
- [ ] **D.** Leave fog lights on in case fog returns

473 You forget to switch off your rear fog lights when the fog has cleared. This may

Mark three answers **NI**

- [x] **A.** Dazzle other road users ✓
- [ ] **B.** Reduce battery life
- [x] **C.** Cause brake lights to be less clear
- [x] **D.** Be breaking the law
- [ ] **E.** Seriously affect engine power

474 You have been driving in thick fog which has now cleared. You must switch OFF your rear fog lights because

Mark one answer **NI**

- [ ] **A.** They use a lot of power from the battery
- [✓] **B.** They make your brake lights less clear
- [ ] **C.** They will cause dazzle in your rear view mirrors ✓
- [ ] **D.** They may not be properly adjusted

475 Front and rear fog lights MUST be

Mark one answer

- [ ] **A.** Connected to an audible warning signal
- [ ] **B.** Used outside built up areas only
- [ ] **C.** Switched off in night-time fog
- [✓] **D.** Switched off if visibility is not seriously reduced ✓

476 You are driving with your front fog lights switched on. Earlier fog has now cleared. What should you do?

Mark one answer

- [ ] **A.** Leave them on if other drivers have their lights on
- [✓] **B.** Switch them off as long as visibility remains good ✓
- [ ] **C.** Flash them to warn oncoming traffic that it is foggy
- [ ] **D.** Drive with them on instead of your headlights

477 While you are driving in fog, it becomes necessary to use front fog lights. You should

Mark one answer

- [ ] **A.** Only turn them on in heavy traffic conditions
- [ ] **B.** Remember not to use them on motorways
- [ ] **C.** Only use them at night
- [✓] **D.** Remember to switch them off as visibility improves ✓

478 You have to park on the road in fog. You should

Mark one answer

- [✓] **A.** Leave sidelights on ✓
- [ ] **B.** Leave dipped headlights and fog lights on
- [ ] **C.** Leave dipped headlights on
- [ ] **D.** Leave main beam headlights on

479 On a foggy day you unavoidably have to park your car on the road. You should

Mark one answer
- [ ] **A.** Leave your headlights on
- [ ] **B.** Leave your fog lights on
- [x] **C.** Leave your sidelights on ✓
- [ ] **D.** Leave your hazard lights on

480 You are driving on a motorway in fog. The left-hand edge of the motorway can be identified by reflective studs. What colour are they?

Mark one answer
- [ ] **A.** Green
- [ ] **B.** Amber
- [x] **C.** Red ✓
- [ ] **D.** White

481 Should lights be used when travelling at night on a well-lit motorway?

Mark one answer
- [ ] **A.** Yes, but only sidelights are needed
- [x] **B.** Yes, dipped headlights are needed ✓
- [ ] **C.** No, unless the weather is bad
- [ ] **D.** No, lights are not needed

482 You are driving on a well-lit motorway at night. You must

Mark one answer
- [ ] **A.** Use only your sidelights
- [x] **B.** Always use your headlights ✓
- [ ] **C.** Always use rear fog lights
- [ ] **D.** Use headlights only in bad weather

483 You are driving on a motorway at night. You MUST have your headlights switched on unless

Mark one answer
- [ ] **A.** There are vehicles close in front of you
- [ ] **B.** You are travelling below 50mph
- [ ] **C.** The motorway is lit
- [x] **D.** Your vehicle is broken down on the hard shoulder ✓

484 You are travelling on a motorway at night with other vehicles just ahead of you. Which lights should you have on?

Mark one answer
- [ ] **A.** Front fog lights
- [ ] **B.** Main beam headlights
- [ ] **C.** Sidelights only
- [x] **D.** Dipped headlights ✓

485 Which TWO of the following are correct? When overtaking at night you should

Mark two answers
- [ ] **A.** Wait until a bend so that you can see the oncoming headlights
- [ ] **B.** Sound your horn twice before moving out
- [x] **C.** Be careful because you can see less ✓
- [x] **D.** Beware of bends in the road ahead ✓
- [ ] **E.** Put headlights on full beam

486 You are overtaking a car at night. You must be sure that

Mark one answer

- **A.** You flash your headlamps before overtaking
- **B.** Your rear fog lights are switched on
- **C.** You have switched your lights to full beam before overtaking
- ☑ **D.** You do not dazzle other road users ✓

487 You are travelling at night. You are dazzled by headlights coming towards you. You should

Mark one answer

- **A.** Pull down your sun visor ✓
- ☑ **B.** Slow down or stop
- **C.** Switch on your main beam headlights
- **D.** Put your hand over your eyes

488 You are dazzled by oncoming headlights when driving at night. What should you do?

Mark one answer

- ☑ **A.** Slow down or stop ✓
- **B.** Brake hard
- **C.** Drive faster past the oncoming car
- **D.** Flash your lights

489 You are parking on a two-way road at night. The speed limit is 40mph. You should park on the

Mark one answer

- ☑ **A.** Left with sidelights on ✓
- **B.** Left with no lights on
- **C.** Right with sidelights on
- **D.** Right with dipped headlights on

490 You are on a narrow road at night. A slower-moving vehicle ahead has been signalling right for some time. What should you do?

Mark one answer

- **A.** Overtake on the left
- **B.** Flash your headlights before overtaking
- **C.** Signal right and sound your horn
- ☑ **D.** Wait for the signal to be cancelled before overtaking ✓

491 A rumble device is designed to

Mark two answers

- **A.** Give directions
- **B.** Prevent cattle escaping
- **C.** Alert drivers to low tyre pressure
- ☑ **D.** Alert drivers to a hazard
- ☑ **E.** Encourage drivers to reduce speed ✓

492 Which TWO are correct? The passing places on a single-track road are

Mark two answers

- **A.** For taking a rest from driving
- ☑ **B.** To pull into if an oncoming vehicle wants to proceed ✓
- **C.** For stopping and checking your route
- **D.** To turn the car around in, if you are lost
- ☑ **E.** To pull into if the car behind wants to overtake ✓

493 You see a vehicle coming towards you on a single-track road. You should

Mark one answer
- **A.** Reverse back to the main road
- ☑ **C.** Stop at a passing place ✓
- **B.** Do an emergency stop
- **D.** Put on your hazard warning lights

Mark four answers
- ☑ **A.** It could be more difficult in winter ✓
- ☑ **B.** Use a low gear and drive slowly ✓
- **C.** Use a high gear to prevent wheelspin
- ☑ **D.** Test your brakes afterwards ✓
- **E.** Always switch on fog lamps
- ☑ **F.** There may be a depth gauge ✓

494 When may you wait in a box junction?

Mark one answer
- **A.** When you are stationary in a queue of traffic
- **B.** When approaching a pelican crossing
- **C.** When approaching a zebra crossing
- ☑ **D.** When oncoming traffic prevents you turning right ✓

496 Which of these plates normally appears with this road sign ?

Mark one answer

☑ **A.** ✓

| Humps for ½ mile |

B.

| Hump Bridge |

C.

| Low Bridge |

D.

| Soft Verge |

495 Which of the following may apply when dealing with this hazard?

497 Which of the following CAN travel on a motorway?

Mark one answer

- [ ] **A.** Cyclists
- [✓] **B.** Vans ✓
- [ ] **C.** Farm tractors
- [ ] **D.** Learner drivers

498 As a provisional licence-holder you should not drive a car

Mark one answer

- [ ] **A.** Over 50mph
- [ ] **B.** At night
- [✓] **C.** On the motorway ✓
- [ ] **D.** With passengers in rear seats

499 Which FOUR of these must not use motorways?

Mark four answers

- [✓] **A.** Learner car drivers ✓
- [ ] **B.** Motorcycles over 50cc
- [ ] **C.** Double-decker buses
- [✓] **D.** Farm tractors ✓
- [✓] **E.** Horse riders ✓
- [✓] **F.** Cyclists ✓

500 Why is it particularly important to carry out a check on your vehicle before making a long motorway journey?

Mark one answer

- [ ] **A.** You will have to do more harsh braking on motorways
- [ ] **B.** Motorway service stations do not deal with breakdowns
- [ ] **C.** The road surface will wear down the tyres faster
- [✓] **D.** Continuous high speeds may increase the risk of your vehicle breaking down ✓

501 Immediately after joining a motorway you should normally

Mark one answer

- [ ] **A.** Try to overtake
- [ ] **B.** Readjust your mirrors
- [ ] **C.** Position your vehicle in the centre lane
- [✓] **D.** Keep in the left lane ✓

502 You are joining a motorway. Why is it important to make full use of the slip road?

Mark one answer

- [ ] **A.** Because there is space available to reverse if you need to
- [ ] **B.** To allow you direct access to the over-taking lanes
- [✓] **C.** To build up a speed similar to traffic on the motorway ✓
- [ ] **D.** Because you can continue on the hard shoulder

503 When joining a motorway you must always

Mark one answer
- **A.** Use the hard shoulder
- **B.** Stop at the end of the acceleration lane
- **C.** Come to a stop before joining the motorway
- ☑ **D.** Give way to traffic already on the motorway ✓

504 You have just joined a motorway. Which lane would you normally stay in to get used to the higher speeds?

Mark one answer
- **A.** Hard shoulder
- **B.** Right-hand lane
- **C.** Centre lane
- ☑ **D.** Left-hand lane ✓

505 What is the national speed limit for cars and motorcycles in the centre lane of a three-lane motorway?

Mark one answer
- **A.** 40mph
- **B.** 50mph
- **C.** 60mph
- ☑ **D.** 70mph

506 What is the national speed limit on motorways for cars and motorcycles?

Mark one answer
- **A.** 30mph
- **B.** 50mph
- **C.** 60mph
- ☑ **D.** 70mph ✓

507 You are towing a trailer on a motorway. What is your maximum speed limit?

Mark one answer
- **A.** 40mph
- **B.** 50mph
- ☑ **C.** 60mph ✓
- **D.** 70mph

508 You are driving a car on a motorway. Unless signs show otherwise you must NOT exceed

Mark one answer
- **A.** 50mph
- **B.** 60mph
- ☑ **C.** 70mph ✓
- **D.** 80mph

509 On a three-lane motorway, which lane should you use for normal driving?

Mark one answer
- ☑ **A.** Left
- **B.** Right
- **C.** Centre
- **D.** Either the right or centre

510 A basic rule when driving on motorways is

Mark one answer
- **A.** Use the lane that has least traffic
- ☑ **B.** Keep to the left lane unless overtaking
- **C.** Overtake on the side that is most clear
- **D.** Try to keep above 50mph to prevent congestion

511 You are driving on a three-lane motorway at 70mph. There is no traffic ahead. Which lane should you use?

Mark one answer

☐ **A.** Any lane
☐ **B.** Middle lane
☐ **C.** Right lane
☑ **D.** Left lane ✓

512 The left-hand lane on a three-lane motorway is for use by

Mark one answer

☑ **A.** Any vehicle ✓
☐ **B.** Large vehicles only
☐ **C.** Emergency vehicles only
☐ **D.** Slow vehicles only

513 The left-hand lane of a motorway should be used for

Mark one answer

☐ **A.** Breakdowns and emergencies only
☐ **B.** Overtaking slower traffic in the other lanes
☐ **C.** Slow vehicles only
☑ **D.** Normal driving ✓

514 What is the right-hand lane used for on a three-lane motorway?

Mark one answer

☐ **A.** Emergency vehicles only
☑ **B.** Overtaking ✓
☐ **C.** Vehicles towing trailers
☐ **D.** Coaches only

515 Which of these IS NOT allowed to travel in the right-hand lane of a three-lane motorway?

Mark one answer

☐ **A.** A small delivery van
☐ **B.** A motorcycle
☑ **C.** A vehicle towing a trailer ✓
☐ **D.** A motorcycle and side-car

516 For what reason may you use the right-hand lane of a motorway?

Mark one answer

☐ **A.** For keeping out of the way of lorries
☐ **B.** For driving at more than 70mph
☐ **C.** For turning right
☑ **D.** For overtaking other vehicles ✓

517 On motorways you should never overtake on the left UNLESS

Mark one answer

- [ ] **A.** You can see well ahead that the hard shoulder is clear
- [ ] **B.** The traffic in the right-hand lane is signalling right
- [ ] **C.** You warn drivers behind by signalling left
- [✓] **D.** There is a queue of traffic to your right that is moving more slowly

518 On a motorway you may ONLY stop on the hard shoulder

Mark one answer

- [✓] **A.** In an emergency
- [ ] **B.** If you feel tired and need to rest
- [ ] **C.** If you accidentally go past the exit that you wanted to take
- [ ] **D.** To pick up a hitchhiker

519 You are travelling on a motorway. You decide you need a rest. You should

Mark two answers

- [ ] **A.** Stop on the hard shoulder
- [✓] **B.** Go to a service area
- [ ] **C.** Park on the slip road
- [ ] **D.** Park on the central reservation
- [✓] **E.** Leave at the next exit

520 You are driving on a motorway. The car ahead shows its hazard lights for a short time. This tells you that

Mark one answer

- [ ] **A.** The driver wants you to overtake
- [ ] **B.** The other car is going to change lanes
- [✓] **C.** Traffic ahead is slowing or stopping suddenly
- [ ] **D.** There is a police speed check ahead

521 You are driving on a motorway. You have to slow down quickly due to a hazard. You should

Mark one answer

- [✓] **A.** Switch on your hazard lights
- [ ] **B.** Switch on your headlights
- [ ] **C.** Sound your horn
- [ ] **D.** Flash your headlights

522 Which vehicles are normally fitted with amber flashing beacons on the roof?

Mark two answers

- [ ] **A.** Doctor's car
- [ ] **B.** Bomb disposal team
- [ ] **C.** Blood transfusion team
- [x] **D.** Breakdown recovery vehicles ✓
- [ ] **E.** Coastguard
- [x] **F.** Maintenance vehicles

523 You break down on a motorway. You need to call for help. Why may it be better to use an emergency roadside telephone rather than a mobile phone?

Mark one answer **NI**

- [ ] **A.** It connects you to a local garage
- [ ] **B.** Using a mobile phone will distract other drivers
- [x] **C.** It allows easy location by the emergency services ✓
- [ ] **D.** Mobile phones do not work on motorways

524 Your vehicle breaks down on the hard shoulder of a motorway. You decide to use your mobile phone to call for help. You should

Mark one answer **NI**

- [ ] **A.** Stand at the rear of the vehicle while making the call
- [ ] **B.** Try to repair the vehicle yourself
- [ ] **C.** Get out of the vehicle by the right hand door
- [x] **D.** Check your location from the marker posts on the left ✓

525 You get a puncture on the motorway. You manage to get your vehicle onto the hard shoulder. You should

Mark one answer

- [ ] **A.** Change the wheel yourself immediately
- [x] **B.** Use the emergency telephone and call for assistance ✓
- [ ] **C.** Try to wave down another vehicle for help
- [ ] **D.** Only change the wheel if you have a passenger to help you

526 The emergency telephones on a motorway are connected to the

Mark one answer

- [ ] **A.** Ambulance service
- [x] **B.** Police control ✓
- [ ] **C.** Fire brigade
- [ ] **D.** Breakdown service

527 How should you use the emergency telephone on a motorway?

Mark one answer

- [ ] **A.** Stay close to the carriageway
- [x] **B.** Face the oncoming traffic ✓
- [ ] **C.** Keep your back to the traffic
- [ ] **D.** Keep your head in the kiosk

528 What should you use the hard shoulder of a motorway for?

Mark one answer
- ☑ **A.** Stopping in an emergency ✓
- ☐ **B.** Leaving the motorway
- ☐ **C.** Stopping when you are tired
- ☐ **D.** Joining the motorway

529 After a breakdown you need to rejoin the main carriageway of a motorway from the hard shoulder. You should

Mark one answer
- ☐ **A.** Move out onto the carriageway then build up your speed ✓
- ☐ **B.** Move out onto the carriageway using your hazard lights
- ☑ **C.** Gain speed on the hard shoulder before moving out onto the carriageway
- ☐ **D.** Wait on the hard shoulder until someone flashes their headlights at you

530 A crawler lane on a motorway is found

Mark one answer
- ☑ **A.** On a steep gradient
- ☐ **B.** Before a service area
- ☐ **C.** Before a junction
- ☐ **D.** Along the hard shoulder

531 Your vehicle has broken down on a motorway. You are not able to stop on the hard shoulder. What should you do?

Mark one answer
- ☑ **A.** Switch on your hazard warning lights
- ☐ **B.** Stop following traffic and ask for help
- ☐ **C.** Attempt to repair your vehicle quickly
- ☐ **D.** Place a warning triangle in the road

532 When may you stop on a motorway?

Mark three answers
- ☐ **A.** If you have to read a map
- ☐ **B.** When you are tired and need a rest
- ☑ **C.** If red lights show above every lane ✓
- ☑ **D.** When told to by the police ✓
- ☐ **E.** If a child in the car feels ill
- ☑ **F.** In an emergency or a breakdown ✓

533 You are allowed to stop on a motorway when you

Mark one answer

- **A.** Need to walk and get fresh air
- **B.** Wish to pick up hitch hikers
- ☑ **C.** Are told to do so by flashing red lights ✓
- **D.** Need to use a mobile telephone

534 You are driving on a motorway. There are red flashing lights above every lane. You must

Mark one answer

- **A.** Pull onto the hard shoulder
- **B.** Slow down and watch for further signals
- **C.** Leave at the next exit
- ☑ **D.** Stop and wait

535 You are driving in the right-hand lane on a motorway. You see these overhead signs. This means

Mark one answer

- ☑ **A.** Move to the left and reduce your speed to 50mph ✓
- **B.** There are roadworks 50 metres (55 yards) ahead
- **C.** Use the hard shoulder untill you have passed the hazard
- **D.** Leave the motorway at the next exit

536 The minimum safe time gap to keep between you and the vehicle in front in good conditions is at least

Mark one answer

- **A.** Four seconds
- **B.** One second
- **C.** Three seconds
- ☑ **D.** Two seconds ✓

537 When driving through a contraflow system on a motorway you should

Mark one answer

- **A.** Ensure that you do not exceed 30mph, for safety
- ☑ **B.** Keep a good distance from the vehicle ahead, for safety
- **C.** Switch lanes to keep the traffic flowing
- **D.** Drive close to the vehicle ahead to reduce queues

538 You are intending to leave the motorway at the next exit. Before you reach the exit you should normally position your vehicle

Mark one answer

- [ ] **A.** In the middle lane
- [x] **B.** In the left-hand lane ✓
- [ ] **C.** On the hard shoulder
- [ ] **D.** In any lane

539 What do these motorway signs show?

Mark one answer

- [ ] **A.** They are countdown markers to a bridge
- [ ] **B.** They are distance markers to the next telephone
- [x] **C.** They are countdown markers to the next exit ✓
- [ ] **D.** They warn of a police control ahead

540 At night, when leaving a well-lit motorway service area, you should

Mark one answer

- [ ] **A.** Drive for some time using only your sidelights
- [x] **B.** Give your eyes time to adjust to the darkness
- [ ] **C.** Switch on your interior light until your eyes adjust
- [ ] **D.** Close your eyes for a moment before leaving the slip road

541 You are driving on a motorway. By mistake, you go past the exit that you wanted to take. You should

Mark one answer

- [ ] **A.** Carefully reverse on the hard shoulder
- [x] **B.** Carry on to the next exit ✓
- [ ] **C.** Carefully reverse in the left-hand lane
- [ ] **D.** Make a U-turn at the next gap in the central reservation

542 On a motorway the amber reflective studs can be found between

Mark one answer

- [ ] **A.** The hard shoulder and the carriageway
- [ ] **B.** The acceleration lane and the carriageway
- [x] **C.** The central reservation and the carriageway ✓
- [ ] **D.** Each pair of the lanes

543 What colour are the reflective studs between the lanes on a motorway?

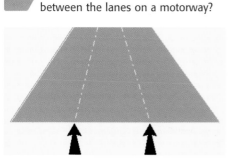

Mark one answer

- [ ] **A.** Green
- [ ] **B.** Amber
- [x] **C.** White ✓
- [ ] **D.** Red

544 You are driving on a three-lane motorway. There are red reflective studs on your left and white ones to your right. Where are you?

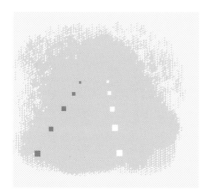

Mark one answer

- [ ] **A.** In the right-hand lane
- [ ] **B.** In the middle lane
- [ ] **C.** On the hard shoulder
- [x] **D.** In the left-hand lane ✓

545 What colour are the reflective studs between a motorway and its slip road?

Mark one answer

- [ ] **A.** Amber
- [ ] **B.** White
- [x] **C.** Green ✓
- [ ] **D.** Red

546 You are travelling on a motorway. What colour are the reflective studs on the left of the carriageway?

Mark one answer

- [ ] **A.** Green
- [x] **B.** Red ✓
- [ ] **C.** White
- [ ] **D.** Amber

547 You may drive over a footpath

Mark one answer
- **A.** To overtake slow-moving traffic
- **B.** When the pavement is very wide
- **C.** If no pedestrians are near
- ✓ **D.** To get into a property ✓

548 What is the meaning of this sign?

Mark one answer
- **A.** Local speed limit applies
- **B.** No waiting on the carriageway
- ✓ **C.** National speed limit applies ✓
- **D.** No entry to vehicular traffic

549 What is the national speed limit on a single carriageway road for cars and motorcycles?

Mark one answer
- **A.** 70mph
- ✓ **B.** 60mph ✓
- **C.** 50mph
- **D.** 30mph

550 What is the national speed limit for cars and motorcycles on a dual carriageway?

Mark one answer
- **A.** 30mph
- **B.** 50mph
- **C.** 60mph ✓
- ✓ **D.** 70mph

551 A single carriageway road has this sign. What is the maximum permitted speed for a car towing a trailer?

Mark one answer
- **A.** 30mph
- **B.** 40mph
- ✓ **C.** 50mph
- **D.** 60mph

552 You are driving along a road that has no traffic signs. There are street lights. What is the speed limit?

Mark one answer
- **A.** 20mph
- ✓ **B.** 30mph ✓
- **C.** 40mph
- **D.** 60mph

553 There are no speed limit signs on the road. How is a 30mph limit indicated?

Mark one answer
- [ ] **A.** By hazard warning lines
- [✓] **B.** By street lighting ✓
- [ ] **C.** By pedestrian islands
- [ ] **D.** By double or single yellow lines

554 Where you see street lights but no speed limit signs the limit is usually

Mark one answer
- [✓] **A.** 30mph ✓
- [ ] **B.** 40mph
- [ ] **C.** 50mph
- [ ] **D.** 60mph

555 You see this sign ahead of you. It means

Mark one answer
- [ ] **A.** Start to slow down to 30mph after passing it
- [ ] **B.** You are leaving the 30mph speed limit area
- [✓] **C.** Do not exceed 30mph after passing it ✓
- [ ] **D.** The minimum speed limit ahead is 30mph

556 If you see a 30mph limit ahead it means

Mark one answer
- [ ] **A.** That the restriction applies only during the working day
- [✓] **B.** That you must not exceed this speed ✓
- [ ] **C.** That it is a guide and you are allowed to drive 10% faster
- [ ] **D.** That you must keep your speed up to 30mph

557 What does a speed limit sign like this mean?

Mark one answer
- [ ] **A.** It is safe to drive at the speed shown
- [ ] **B.** The speed shown is the advised maximum
- [ ] **C.** The speed shown allows for various road and weather conditions
- [✓] **D.** You must not exceed the speed shown ✓

558 You are towing a small caravan on a dual carriageway. You must not exceed

Mark one answer
- ☑ **A.** 50mph
- ☐ **B.** 40mph
- ☐ **C.** 70mph
- ☑ **D.** 60mph

559 What does this sign mean?

Mark one answer
- ☐ **A.** Minimum speed 30mph
- ☐ **B.** End of maximum speed
- ☑ **C.** End of minimum speed
- ☐ **D.** Maximum speed 30mph

560 You are driving along a street with parked vehicles on the left-hand side. For which THREE reasons should you keep your speed down?

Mark three answers
- ☐ **A.** So that oncoming traffic can see you more clearly
- ☐ **B.** You may set off car alarms
- ☑ **C.** Vehicles may be pulling out
- ☑ **D.** Drivers' doors may open
- ☑ **E.** Children may run out from between the vehicles

561 You meet an obstruction on your side of the road. You should

Mark one answer
- ☐ **A.** Drive on: it is your right of way
- ☑ **B.** Give way to oncoming traffic
- ☐ **C.** Wave oncoming vehicles through
- ☐ **D.** Accelerate to get past first

562 There is a tractor ahead of you. You wish to overtake but you are NOT sure if it is safe to do so. You should

Mark one answer
- ☐ **A.** Follow another overtaking vehicle through
- ☐ **B.** Sound your horn to the slow vehicle to pull over
- ☐ **C.** Speed through but flash your lights to oncoming traffic
- ☑ **D.** Not overtake if you are in doubt

563 Which three of the following are most likely to take an unusual course at roundabouts?

Mark three answers
- ☑ **A.** Horse riders
- ☐ **B.** Milk floats
- ☐ **C.** Delivery vans
- ☑ **D.** Long vehicles
- ☐ **E.** Estate cars
- ☑ **F.** Cyclists

564 You are leaving your vehicle parked on a road. When may you leave the engine running?

Mark one answer
- **A.** If you will be parked for less than five minutes
- **B.** If the battery is flat
- **C.** When in a 20mph zone
- ☑ **D.** Not on any occasion ✓

565 In which FOUR places must you NOT park or wait?

Mark four answers
- **A.** On a dual carriageway
- ☑ **B.** At a bus stop ✓
- **C.** On the slope of a hill
- ☑ **D.** Opposite a traffic island ✓
- ☑ **E.** In front of someone else's drive ✓
- ☑ **F.** On the brow of a hill ✓

566 What is the nearest you may park your vehicle to a junction?

Mark one answer **NI**
- ☑ **A.** 10 metres (33 feet) ✓
- **B.** 12 metres (39 feet)
- **C.** 15 metres (49 feet)
- **D.** 20 metres (66 feet)

567 You are finding it difficult to find a parking place in a busy town. You can see there is space on the zigzag lines of a zebra crossing. Can you park there?

Mark one answer
- **A.** No, unless you stay with your car
- **B.** Yes, in order to drop off a passenger ╱
- **C.** Yes, if you do not block people from crossing
- ☑ **D.** No, not in any circumstances ─

568 In which TWO places must you NOT park?

Mark two answers
- ☑ **A.** Near a school entrance ✓
- **B.** Near a police station
- **C.** In a side road
- ☑ **D.** At a bus stop ✓
- **E.** In a one-way street

569 In which THREE places must you NOT park your vehicle?

Mark three answers **NI**
- ☑ **A.** Near the brow of a hill ✓
- ☑ **B.** At or near a bus stop ✓
- **C.** Where there is no pavement
- ☑ **D.** Within 10 metres (33 feet) of a junction ✓
- **E.** On a 40mph road

570 On a clearway you must not stop

Mark one answer
- ☑ **A.** At any time ✓
- **B.** When it is busy
- **C.** In the rush hour
- **D.** During daylight hours

571 You are driving on an urban clearway. You may stop only to

Mark one answer
- [✓] **A.** Set down and pick up passengers ✓
- [ ] **B.** Use a mobile telephone
- [ ] **C.** Ask for directions
- [ ] **D.** Load or unload goods

572 You want to park and you see this sign. On the days and times shown you should

Meter ZONE

Mon - Fri
8.30 am - 6.30 pm
Saturday
8.30 am - 1.30 pm

Mark one answer
- [ ] **A.** Park in a bay and not pay
- [ ] **B.** Park on yellow lines and pay
- [ ] **C.** Park on yellow lines and not pay
- [✓] **D.** Park in a bay and pay ✓

573 What is the meaning of this sign?

Mark one answer
- [ ] **A.** No entry
- [✓] **B.** Waiting restrictions ✓
- [ ] **C.** National speed limit
- [ ] **D.** School crossing patrol

574 What MUST you have to park in a disabled space?

DISABLED

Mark one answer
- [✓] **A.** An orange badge ✓
- [ ] **B.** A wheelchair
- [ ] **C.** An advanced driver certificate
- [ ] **D.** A modified vehicle

575 You are looking for somewhere to park your vehicle. The area is full EXCEPT for spaces marked 'disabled use'. You can

Mark one answer
- [ ] **A.** Use these spaces when elsewhere is full
- [ ] **B.** Park if you stay with your vehicle
- [ ] **C.** Use these spaces, disabled or not
- [✓] **D.** Not park there unless permitted ✓

576 Your vehicle is parked on the road at night. When must you use sidelights?

Mark one answer
- ☐ **A.** Where there are continuous white lines in the middle of the road
- ☑ **B.** Where the speed limit exceeds 30mph ✓
- ☐ **C.** Where you are facing oncoming traffic
- ☐ **D.** Where you are near a bus stop

577 You park overnight on a road with a 40mph speed limit. You should

Mark one answer
- ☐ **A.** Park facing the traffic
- ☑ **B.** Park with sidelights on ✓
- ☐ **C.** Park with dipped headlights on
- ☐ **D.** Park near a street light

578 You can park on the right-hand side of a road at night

Mark one answer
- ☑ **A.** In a one-way street ✓
- ☐ **B.** With your sidelights on
- ☐ **C.** More than 10 metres (33 feet) from a junction
- ☐ **D.** Under a lamp-post

579 On a three-lane dual carriageway the right-hand lane can be used for

580 You are driving at night with full beam headlights on. A vehicle is overtaking you. You should dip your lights

Mark one answer
- ☐ **A.** Overtaking only, never turning right
- ☑ **B.** Overtaking or turning right ✓
- ☐ **C.** Fast-moving traffic only
- ☐ **D.** Turning right only, never overtaking

580 You are driving at night with full beam headlights on. A vehicle is overtaking you. You should dip your lights

Mark one answer
- ☐ **A.** Some time after the vehicle has passed you
- ☐ **B.** Before the vehicle starts to pass you
- ☐ **C.** Only if the other driver dips his headlights
- ☑ **D.** As soon as the vehicle passes you

581 You are driving on a two-lane dual carriageway. For which TWO of the following would you use the right-hand lane?

Mark two answers
- ☑ **A.** Turning right ✓
- ☐ **B.** Normal driving
- ☐ **C.** Driving at the minimum allowed speed
- ☐ **D.** Constant high-speed driving
- ☑ **E.** Overtaking slower traffic ✓
- ☐ **F.** Mending punctures

582 You are driving in the right-hand lane of a dual carriageway. You see signs showing that the right lane is closed 800 yards ahead. You should

GET IN LANE

800 yards

Mark one answer

- [ ] **A.** Keep in that lane until you reach the queue
- [ ] **B.** Move to the left immediately
- [ ] **C.** Wait and see which lane is moving faster
- [x] **D.** Move to the left in good time ✓

583 You are entering an area of roadworks. There is a temporary speed limit displayed. You must

Mark one answer

- [x] **A.** Not exceed the speed limit ✓
- [ ] **B.** Obey the limit only during rush hour
- [ ] **C.** Accept the speed limit as advisable
- [ ] **D.** Obey the limit except for overnight

584 While driving, you approach roadworks. You see a temporary maximum speed limit sign. You must

Mark one answer

- [ ] **A.** Comply with the sign during the working day
- [x] **B.** Comply with the sign at all times ✓
- [ ] **C.** Comply with the sign when the lanes are narrow
- [ ] **D.** Comply with the sign during the hours of darkness

585 You may drive a motor car in this bus lane

local
taxi
Mon - Fri
7 - 10 am
4.00 - 6.30 pm

Mark one answer

- [x] **A.** Outside its operation hours ✓
- [ ] **B.** To get to the front of a traffic queue
- [ ] **C.** At no times at all
- [ ] **D.** To overtake slow moving traffic

586 As a car driver which THREE lanes are you NOT normally allowed to use?

Mark three answers

- [ ] **A.** Crawler lane
- [x] **B.** Bus lane ✓
- [ ] **C.** Overtaking lane
- [ ] **D.** Acceleration lane
- [x] **E.** Cycle lane ✓
- [x] **F.** Tram lane ✓

587 You are driving on a road that has a cycle lane. The lane is marked by a broken white line. This means that

Mark one answer

☑ **A.** You should not drive in the lane unless it is unavoidable

☑ **B.** You should not park in the lane unless it is unavoidable

☐ **C.** You can drive in the lane at any time

☐ **D.** The lane must be used by motorcyclists in heavy traffic

588 You are driving along a road that has a cycle lane. The lane is marked by a solid white line. This means that during its period of operation

Mark one answer

☐ **A.** The lane may be used for parking your car

☐ **B.** You may drive in that lane at any time

☐ **C.** The lane may be used when necessary

☑ **D.** You must not drive in that lane ✓

589 A cycle lane is marked by a solid white line. You must not drive or park in it

Mark one answer

☐ **A.** At any time

☐ **B.** During the rush hour

☐ **C.** If a cyclist is using it

☑ **D.** During its period of operation

590 You are approaching a busy junction. There are several lanes with road markings. At the last moment you realise that you are in the wrong lane. You should

Mark one answer

☑ **A.** Continue in that lane ✓

☐ **B.** Force your way across

☐ **C.** Stop until the area has cleared

☐ **D.** Use clear arm signals to cut across

591 Where may you overtake on a one-way street?

Mark one answer

☐ **A.** Only on the left-hand side

☐ **B.** Overtaking is not allowed

☐ **C.** Only on the right-hand side

☑ **D.** Either on the right or the left ✓

592 You are going along a single-track road with passing places only on the right. The driver behind wishes to overtake. You should

Mark one answer

☐ **A.** Speed up to get away from the following driver

☐ **B.** Switch on your hazard warning lights

☑ **C.** Wait opposite a passing place on your right

☐ **D.** Drive into a passing place on your right

593 You are on a road that is only wide enough for one vehicle. There is a car coming towards you. Which TWO of these would be correct?

Mark two answers

- **A.** Pull into a passing place on your right
- **B.** Force the other driver to reverse
- **C.** Pull into a passing place if your vehicle is wider
- ☑ **D.** Pull into a passing place on your left ✓
- ☑ **E.** Wait opposite a passing place on your right
- **F.** Wait opposite a passing place on your left

594 Signals are normally given by direction indicators and

Mark one answer

- ☑ **A.** Brake lights
- **B.** Side lights
- **C.** Fog lights
- **D.** Interior lights

595 When going straight ahead at a roundabout you should

Mark one answer

- ☑ **A.** Indicate left before leaving the roundabout ✓
- **B.** Not indicate at any time
- **C.** Indicate right when approaching the roundabout
- **D.** Indicate left when approaching the roundabout

596 Which vehicle might have to use a different course to normal at roundabouts?

Mark one answer

- **A.** Sports car
- **B.** Van
- **C.** Estate car
- ☑ **D.** Long vehicle ✓

597 You are going straight ahead at a roundabout. How should you signal?

Mark one answer

- **A.** Signal right on the approach and then left to leave the roundabout
- **B.** Signal left as you leave the roundabout
- **C.** Signal left on the approach to the roundabout and keep the signal on until you leave
- ☑ **D.** Signal left just after you pass the exit before the one you will take

598 At a crossroads there are no signs or road markings. Two vehicles approach. Which has priority?

Mark one answer

- ☑ **A.** Neither vehicle ✓
- **B.** The vehicle travelling the fastest
- **C.** The vehicle on the widest road
- **D.** Vehicles approaching from the right

599 Who has priority at an unmarked crossroads?

Mark one answer

- [ ] **A.** The driver of the larger vehicle
- [✓] **B.** No one ✓
- [ ] **C.** The driver who is going faster
- [ ] **D.** The driver on the wider road

600 You are intending to turn right at a junction. An oncoming driver is also turning right. It will normally be safer to

Mark one answer

- [✓] **A.** Keep the other vehicle to your RIGHT ✓ and turn behind it (offside to offside)
- [ ] **B.** Keep the other vehicle to your LEFT and turn in front of it (nearside to nearside)
- [ ] **C.** Carry on and turn at the next junction instead
- [ ] **D.** Hold back and wait for the other driver to turn first

Безопасен проезд удар

601 The dual carriageway you are turning right onto has a narrow central reserve. You should

Mark one answer

- [ ] **A.** Proceed to central reserve and wait
- [✓] **B.** Wait until the road is clear in both directions
- [ ] **C.** Stop in first lane so that other vehicles give way
- [ ] **D.** Emerge slightly to show your intentions

602 While driving, you intend to turn left into a minor road. On the approach you should

Mark one answer

- [ ] **A.** Keep just left of the middle of the road
- [ ] **B.** Keep in the middle of the road
- [ ] **C.** Swing out wide just before turning
- [✓] **D.** Keep well to the left of the road

603 You may only enter a box junction when

Mark one answer

- [ ] **A.** There are less than two vehicles in front of you
- [ ] **B.** The traffic lights show green
- [✓] **C.** Your exit road is clear ✓
- [ ] **D.** You need to turn left ·

604 You may wait in a yellow box junction when

Mark one answer

- [✓] **A.** Oncoming traffic is preventing you from turning right ✓
- [ ] **B.** You are in a queue of traffic turning left
- [ ] **C.** You are in a queue of traffic to go ahead
- [ ] **D.** You are on a roundabout

605 You want to turn right at a box junction. There is oncoming traffic. You should

Mark one answer

- ☑ **A.** Wait in the box junction if your exit is clear ✓
- ☐ **B.** Wait before the junction until it is clear of all traffic
- ☐ **C.** Drive on: you cannot turn right at a box junction
- ☐ **D.** Drive slowly into the box junction when signalled by oncoming traffic

606 On which THREE occasions MUST you stop your vehicle?

Mark three answers

- ☑ **A.** When involved in an accident ✓
- ☑ **B.** At a red traffic light ✓
- ☑ **C.** When signalled to do so by a police officer ✓
- ☐ **D.** At a junction with double broken white lines
- ☐ **E.** At a pelican crossing when the amber light is flashing and no pedestrians are crossing

607 You MUST stop when signalled to do so by which THREE of these?

Mark three answers

- ☑ **A.** A police officer ✓
- ☐ **B.** A pedestrian
- ☑ **C.** A school crossing patrol ✓
- ☐ **D.** A bus driver
- ☑ **E.** A red traffic light ✓

608 At roadworks which of the following can control traffic flow?

Mark three answers

- ☑ **A.** A STOP-GO board ✓
- ☐ **B.** Flashing amber lights
- ☑ **C.** A policeman
- ☐ **D.** Flashing red lights
- ☑ **E.** Temporary traffic lights ✓

609 You are waiting at a level crossing. The red warning lights continue to flash after a train has passed by. What should you do?

Mark one answer

- ☐ **A.** Get out and investigate
- ☐ **B.** Telephone the signal operator
- ☑ **C.** Continue to wait ✓
- ☐ **D.** Drive across carefully

610 You are driving over a level crossing. The warning lights come on and a bell rings. What should you do?

Mark one answer

A. Get everyone out of the vehicle immediately

B. Stop and reverse back to clear the crossing

☑ C. Keep going and clear the crossing ✓

D. Stop immediately and use your hazard warning lights

611 You are waiting at a level crossing. A train has passed but the lights keep flashing. You must

Mark one answer

☑ A. Carry on waiting ✓

B. Phone the signal operator

C. Edge over the stop line and look for trains

D. Park your vehicle and investigate

612 You will see these markers when approaching

Mark one answer

A. The end of a motorway

☑ B. A concealed level crossing ✓

C. A concealed speed limit sign

D. The end of a dual carriageway

613 Someone is waiting to cross at a zebra crossing. They are standing on the pavement. You should normally

Mark one answer

A. Go on quickly before they step onto the crossing

B. Stop before you reach the zigzag lines and let them cross

☑ C. Stop, let them cross, wait patiently ✓

D. Ignore them as they are still on the pavement

614 At toucan crossings, apart from pedestrians you should be aware of

Mark one answer

A. Emergency vehicles emerging

B. Buses pulling out

C. Trams crossing in front

☑ D. Cyclists riding across ✓

615 Who can use a toucan crossing?

Mark two answers
- [ ] **A.** Trains
- [x] **B.** Cyclists ✓
- [ ] **C.** Buses
- [x] **D.** Pedestrians ✓
- [ ] **E.** Trams

616 At a pelican crossing, what does a flashing amber light mean?

Mark one answer
- [ ] **A.** You must not move off until the lights stop flashing
- [x] **B.** You must give way to pedestrians still on the crossing ✓
- [ ] **C.** You can move off, even if pedestrians are still on the crossing
- [ ] **D.** You must stop because the lights are about to change to red

617 You are waiting at a pelican crossing. The red light changes to flashing amber. This means you must

Mark one answer
- [x] **A.** Wait for pedestrians on the crossing to clear ✓
- [ ] **B.** Move off immediately without any hesitation
- [ ] **C.** Wait for the green light before moving off
- [ ] **D.** Get ready and go when the continuous amber light shows

618 You are on a busy main road and find that you are travelling in the wrong direction. What should you do?

Mark one answer
- [ ] **A.** Turn into a side road on the right and reverse into the main road
- [ ] **B.** Make a U-turn in the main road
- [ ] **C.** Make a three-point turn in the main road
- [x] **D.** Turn round in a side road ✓

619 You may remove your seat belt when carrying out a manoeuvre that involves

Mark one answer
- [x] **A.** Reversing ✓
- [ ] **B.** A hill start
- [ ] **C.** An emergency stop
- [ ] **D.** Driving slowly

620 You must not reverse

Mark one answer
- [x] **A.** For longer than necessary ✓
- [ ] **B.** For more than a car's length
- [ ] **C.** Into a side road
- [ ] **D.** In a built-up area

621 You are parked in a busy high street. What is the safest way to turn your vehicle around to go the opposite way?

Mark one answer

- ✓ **A.** Find a quiet side road to turn round in ✓
- **B.** Drive into a side road and reverse into the main road
- **C.** Get someone to stop the traffic
- **D.** Do a U-turn

622 When you are NOT sure that it is safe to reverse your vehicle you should

Mark one answer

- **A.** Use your horn
- **B.** Rev your engine
- ✓ **C.** Get out and check ✓
- **D.** Reverse slowly

623 When may you reverse from a side road into a main road?

Mark one answer

- **A.** Only if both roads are clear of traffic
- ✓ **B.** Not at any time ✓
- **C.** At any time
- **D.** Only if the main road is clear of traffic

624 You are reversing your vehicle into a side road. When would the greatest hazard to passing traffic occur?

Mark one answer

- **A.** After you have completed the manoeuvre
- **B.** Just before you actually begin to manoeuvre
- **C.** After you've entered the side road
- ✓ **D.** When the front of your vehicle swings out

625 You MUST obey signs giving orders. These signs are mostly in

Mark one answer
- **A.** Green rectangles
- **B.** Red triangles
- **C.** Blue rectangles
- ☑ **D.** Red circles ✓

626 Traffic signs giving orders are generally which shape?

Mark one answer
- **A.**
- **B.**
- **C.**
- ☑ **D.** ✓

627 Which type of sign tells you NOT to do something?

Mark one answer
- ☑ **A.** ✓
- **B.**
- **C.**
- **D.**

628 What does this sign mean?

Mark one answer
- ☑ **A.** Maximum speed limit with traffic calming ✓
- **B.** Minimum speed limit with traffic calming
- **C.** 20 cars only parking zone
- **D.** Only 20 cars allowed at any one time

629 Which sign means no motor vehicles are allowed?

Mark one answer
- **A.**
- ☑ **B.** ✓
- **C.**
- **D.**

630 Which of these signs means no motor vehicles?

Mark one answer
- ☑ **A.** ✓
- **B.**
- **C.**
- **D.**

631 What does this sign mean?

Mark one answer
- [ ] **A.** New speed limit 20mph
- [ ] **B.** No vehicles over 30 tonnes
- [ ] **C.** Minimum speed limit 30mph
- [x] **D.** End of 20mph zone ✓

632 This traffic sign means there is

Mark one answer
- [x] **A.** A compulsory maximum speed limit ✓
- [ ] **B.** An advised maximum speed limit
- [ ] **C.** A compulsory minimum speed limit
- [ ] **D.** An advised separation distance

633 What does this sign mean?

Mark one answer
- [ ] **A.** No overtaking
- [x] **B.** No motor vehicles ✓
- [ ] **C.** Clearway (no stopping)
- [ ] **D.** Cars and motorcycles only

634 What does this sign mean?

Mark one answer
- [ ] **A.** No parking
- [ ] **B.** No road markings
- [ ] **C.** No through road
- [x] **D.** No entry ✓

635 What does this sign mean?

Mark one answer
- [ ] **A.** Bend to the right
- [ ] **B.** Road on the right closed
- [ ] **C.** No traffic from the right
- [x] **D.** No right turn ✓

636 Which sign means no entry?

Mark one answer
- [ ] **A.**
- [ ] **B.**
- [ ] **C.**
- [x] **D.** ✓

637 What does this sign mean?

Mark one answer
- [x] **A.** Route for trams only ✓
- [ ] **B.** Route for buses only
- [ ] **C.** Parking for buses only
- [ ] **D.** Parking for trams only

638 Which type of vehicle does this sign apply to?

Mark one answer
- **A.** Wide vehicles
- **B.** Long vehicles
- ☑ **C.** High vehicles ✓
- **D.** Heavy vehicles

639 Which sign means NO motor vehicles allowed?

Mark one answer
- **A.**
- ☑ **B.** ✓
- **C.**
- **D.**

640 What does this sign mean?

Mark one answer
- **A.** You have priority
- **B.** No motor vehicles
- **C.** Two-way traffic
- ☑ **D.** No overtaking ✓

641 What does this sign mean?

Mark one answer
- **A.** Keep in one lane
- **B.** Give way to oncoming traffic
- ☑ **C.** Do not overtake ✓
- **D.** Form two lanes

642 Which sign means no overtaking?

Mark one answer
- **A.**
- ☑ **B.** ✓
- **C.**
- **D.**

643 What does this sign mean?

Mark one answer
- ☑ **A.** Waiting restrictions apply ✓
- **B.** Waiting permitted
- **C.** National speed limit applies
- **D.** Clearway (no stopping)

644 What does this sign mean?

Mark one answer
- **A.** You can park on the days and times shown
- ☑ **B.** No parking on the days and times shown ✓
- **C.** No parking at all from Monday to Friday
- **D.** You can park at any time: the urban clearway ends

645 What does this sign mean?

Mark one answer

- [ ] **A.** End of restricted speed area
- [✓] **B.** End of restricted parking area
- [ ] **C.** End of clearway
- [ ] **D.** End of cycle route

Zone **ENDS**

646 Which sign means no stopping?

Mark one answer

- [ ] **A.**
- [✓] **B.** ✓
- [ ] **C.**
- [ ] **D.**

647 What does this sign mean?

Mark one answer

- [ ] **A.** Roundabout
- [ ] **B.** Crossroads
- [✓] **C.** No stopping ✓
- [ ] **D.** No entry

648 You see this sign ahead. It means

Mark one answer

- [ ] **A.** National speed limit applies
- [ ] **B.** Waiting restrictions apply
- [✓] **C.** No stopping ✓
- [ ] **D.** No entry

649 What does this sign mean?

Mark one answer

- [✓] **A.** Distance to parking place ahead ✓
- [ ] **B.** Distance to public telephone ahead
- [ ] **C.** Distance to public house ahead
- [ ] **D.** Distance to passing place ahead

P
1 mile

650 What does this sign mean?

Mark one answer

- [ ] **A.** Vehicles may not park on the verge or footway
- [ ] **B.** Vehicles may park on the left-hand side of the road only ✓
- [✓] **C.** Vehicles may park fully on the verge or footway
- [ ] **D.** Vehicles may park on the right-hand side of the road only

P

651 What does this traffic sign mean?

Mark one answer

- [ ] **A.** No overtaking allowed
- [✓] **B.** Give priority to oncoming traffic ✓
- [ ] **C.** Two-way traffic
- [ ] **D.** One-way traffic only

652 What is the meaning of this traffic sign?

Mark one answer
- **A.** End of two-way road
- **B.** Give priority to vehicles coming towards you
- ☑ **C.** You have priority over vehicles coming towards you ✓
- **D.** Bus lane ahead

655 What does this sign mean?

Mark one answer
- **A.** No overtaking
- **B.** You are entering a one-way street
- **C.** Two-way traffic ahead
- ☑ **D.** You have priority over vehicles from the opposite direction ✓

653 Which sign means 'traffic has priority over oncoming vehicles'?

Mark one answer
- **A.**
- **B.**
- ☑ **C.** ✓
- **D.**

656 What shape is a STOP sign at a junction?

Mark one answer
- **A.**
- **B.**
- **C.**
- ☑ **D.** ✓

654 What MUST you do when you see this sign?

Mark one answer
- **A.** Stop, ONLY if traffic is approaching
- ☑ **B.** Stop, even if the road is clear ✓
- **C.** Stop, ONLY if children are waiting to cross
- **D.** Stop, ONLY if a red light is showing

657 At a junction you see this sign partly covered by snow. What does it mean?

Mark one answer
- **A.** Crossroads
- **B.** Give way
- ☑ **C.** Stop ✓
- **D.** Turn right

658 Which shape is used for a GIVE WAY sign?

Mark one answer

- [ ] **A.**
- [ ] **B.**
- [ ] **C.**
- [x] **D.** ✓

659 What does this sign mean?

Mark one answer

- [ ] **A.** Service area 30 miles ahead
- [ ] **B.** Maximum speed 30mph
- [x] **C.** Minimum speed 30mph ✓
- [ ] **D.** Lay-by 30 miles ahead

660 Which of these signs means turn left ahead ?

Mark one answer

- [ ] **A.**
- [x] **B.** ✓
- [ ] **C.**
- [ ] **D.**

661 At a mini-roundabout you should

Mark one answer

- [x] **A.** Give way to traffic from the right ✓
- [ ] **B.** Give way to traffic from the left
- [ ] **C.** Give way to traffic from the other way
- [ ] **D.** Stop even when clear

662 What does this sign mean ?

Mark one answer

- [ ] **A.** Buses turning
- [ ] **B.** Ring road
- [x] **C.** Mini-roundabout ✓
- [ ] **D.** Keep right

663 What does this sign mean?

Mark one answer

- [ ] **A.** Give way to oncoming vehicles
- [ ] **B.** Approaching traffic passes you on both sides
- [ ] **C.** Turn off at the next available junction
- [x] **D.** Pass either side to get to the same destination ✓

664 What does this sign mean?

Mark one answer

- [x] **A.** Route for trams ✓
- [ ] **B.** Give way to trams
- [ ] **C.** Route for buses
- [ ] **D.** Give way to buses

Only

665 What does a circular traffic sign with a blue background do?

Mark one answer

- [ ] **A.** Give warning of a motorway ahead
- [ ] **B.** Give directions to a car park
- [ ] **C.** Give motorway information
- [x] **D.** Give an instruction ✓

666 Which of these signs means that you are entering a one-way street?

Mark one answer

A. ☐   B. ☑ ✓   C. ☐   D. ☐

667 Where would you see a contraflow bus and cycle lane?

Mark one answer

☐ A. On a dual carriageway
☐ B. On a roundabout
☐ C. On an urban motorway ✓
☑ D. On a one-way street

668 What does this sign mean?

Mark one answer

☐ A. Bus station on the right
☑ B. Contraflow bus lane ✓
☐ C. With-flow bus lane
☐ D. Give way to buses

669 What does this sign mean?

Mark one answer

☑ A. With-flow bus and cycle lane ✓
☐ B. Contraflow bus and cycle lane
☐ C. No buses and cycles allowed
☐ D. No waiting for buses and cycles

670 What does a sign with a brown background show?

Mark one answer

☑ A. Tourist directions ✓
☐ B. Primary roads
☐ C. Motorway routes
☐ D. Minor routes

671 This sign means

Mark one answer

☑ A. Tourist attraction ✓
☐ B. Beware of trains
☐ C. Level crossing
☐ D. Beware of trams

672 What are triangular signs for?

Mark one answer

☑ A. To give warnings ✓
☐ B. To give information
☐ C. To give orders
☐ D. To give directions

673 What does this sign mean?

Mark one answer
- [ ] **A.** Turn left ahead
- [✓] **B.** T-junction ✓
- [ ] **C.** No through road
- [ ] **D.** Give way

674 What does this sign mean?

Mark one answer
- [ ] **A.** Multi-exit roundabout
- [✓] **B.** Risk of ice ✓
- [ ] **C.** Six roads converge
- [ ] **D.** Place of historical interest

675 What does this sign mean?

Mark one answer
- [✓] **A.** Crossroads ✓
- [ ] **B.** Level crossing with gate
- [ ] **C.** Level crossing without gate
- [ ] **D.** Ahead only

676 What does this sign mean?

Mark one answer
- [ ] **A.** Ring road
- [ ] **B.** Mini-roundabout
- [ ] **C.** No vehicles
- [✓] **D.** Roundabout ✓

677 Which FOUR of these would be indicated by a triangular road sign?

Mark four answers
- [✓] **A.** Road narrows ✓
- [ ] **B.** Ahead only
- [✓] **C.** Low bridge ✓
- [ ] **D.** Minimum speed
- [✓] **E.** Children crossing ✓
- [✓] **F.** T-junction ✓

678 What does this sign mean?

Mark one answer
- [ ] **A.** Cyclists must dismount
- [ ] **B.** Cycles are not allowed
- [✓] **C.** Cycle route ahead ✓
- [ ] **D.** Cycle in single file

679 Which sign means that pedestrians may be walking along the road?

Mark one answer
- [✓] **A.**   [ ] **B.**   [ ] **C.**   [ ] **D.**

680 Which of these signs warn you of a pedestrian crossing?

Mark one answer
- [✓] **A.**   [ ] **B.**   [ ] **C.**   [ ] **D.**

681 What does this sign mean?

Mark one answer
- **A.** No footpath ahead
- **B.** Pedestrians only ahead
- ✓ **C.** Pedestrian crossing ahead ✓
- **D.** School crossing ahead

682 What does this sign mean?

Mark one answer
- **A.** School crossing patrol
- **B.** No pedestrians allowed
- **C.** Pedestrian zone – no vehicles
- ✓ **D.** Pedestrian crossing ahead ✓

683 Which of these signs means there is a double bend ahead?

Mark one answer
- **A.**
- ✓ **B.** ✓
- **C.**
- **D.**

684 What does this sign mean?

Mark one answer
- **A.** Wait at the barriers
- **B.** Wait at the crossroads
- ✓ **C.** Give way to trams ✓
- **D.** Give way to farm vehicles

685 What does this sign mean?

Mark one answer
- **A.** Humpback bridge
- ✓ **B.** Humps in the road ✓
- **C.** Entrance to tunnel
- **D.** Soft verges

686 What does this sign mean?

Mark one answer
- **A.** Low bridge ahead
- ✓ **B.** Tunnel ahead ✓
- **C.** Ancient monument ahead
- **D.** Accident black spot ahead

687 What does this sign mean?

Mark one answer
- **A.** Two-way traffic straight ahead
- ✓ **B.** Two-way traffic crossing a one-way street ✓
- **C.** Two-way traffic over a bridge
- **D.** Two-way traffic crosses a two-way road

688 Which sign means 'two-way traffic crosses a one-way road'?

Mark one answer
- **A.**
- ✓ **B.** ✓
- **C.**
- **D.**

689 Which of these signs means the end of a dual carriageway?

Mark one answer

☐ **A.**   ☐ **B.**   ☐ **C.**   ☑ **D.** ✓

---

690 What does this sign mean?

Mark one answer

☑ **A.** End of dual carriageway ✓
☐ **B.** Tall bridge
☐ **C.** Road narrows
☐ **D.** End of narrow bridge

---

691 What does this sign mean?

Mark one answer

☐ **A.** Two-way traffic ahead across a one-way street
☐ **B.** Traffic approaching you has priority
☑ **C.** Two-way traffic straight ahead ✓
☐ **D.** Motorway contraflow system ahead

---

692 What does this sign mean?

Mark one answer

☑ **A.** Crosswinds ✓
☐ **B.** Road noise
☐ **C.** Airport
☐ **D.** Adverse camber

---

693 What does this traffic sign mean?

Mark one answer

☐ **A.** Slippery road ahead
☐ **B.** Tyres liable to punctures ahead
☑ **C.** Danger ahead ✓
☐ **D.** Service area ahead

---

694 You are about to overtake when you see this sign. You should

Mark one answer

☐ **A.** Overtake the other driver as quickly as possible
☐ **B.** Move to the right to get a better view
☐ **C.** Switch your headlights on before overtaking
☑ **D.** Hold back until you can see clearly ahead ✓

Hidden dip

---

695 What does this sign mean?

Mark one answer

☑ **A.** Level crossing with gate or barrier ✓
☐ **B.** Gated road ahead
☐ **C.** Level crossing without gate or barrier
☐ **D.** Cattle grid ahead

---

696 What does this sign mean?

Mark one answer

☐ **A.** No trams ahead
☐ **B.** Oncoming trams
☑ **C.** Trams crossing ahead ✓
☐ **D.** Trams only

697 What does this sign mean?

Mark one answer
- **A.** Adverse camber
- ☑ **B.** Steep hill downwards ✓
- **C.** Uneven road
- **D.** Steep hill upwards

698 What does this sign mean?

Mark one answer
- ☑ **A.** Quayside or river bank
- **B.** Steep hill downwards
- **C.** Slippery road
- **D.** Road liable to flooding

699 What does this sign mean?

Mark one answer
- **A.** Uneven road surface
- **B.** Bridge over the road
- **C.** Road ahead ends
- ☑ **D.** Water across the road ✓

700 What does this sign mean?

Mark one answer
- ☑ **A.** Humpback bridge ✓
- **B.** Traffic calming hump
- **C.** Low bridge
- **D.** Uneven road

701 What does this sign mean?

Mark one answer
- **A.** Turn left for parking area
- ☑ **B.** No through road on the left ✓
- **C.** No entry for traffic turning left
- **D.** Turn left for ferry terminal

702 What does this sign mean?

Mark one answer
- **A.** T-junction
- ☑ **B.** No through road ✓
- **C.** Telephone box ahead
- **D.** Toilet ahead

703 Which sign means 'no through road'?

Mark one answer
- **A.**
- **B.**
- ☑ **C.** ✓
- **D.**

704 Which of the following signs informs you that you are coming to a No Through Road?

Mark one answer
- **A.**
- **B.**
- ☑ **C.** ✓
- **D.**

705 What does this sign mean?

Mark one answer

- ☑ **A.** Direction to park and ride car park
- ☐ **B.** No parking for buses or coaches
- ☐ **C.** Directions to bus and coach park
- ☐ **D.** Parking area for cars and coaches ✗

706 You are driving through a tunnel and you see this sign. What does it mean?

Mark one answer

- ☑ **A.** Direction to emergency pedestrian exit ✓
- ☐ **B.** Beware of pedestrians, no footpath ahead
- ☐ **C.** No access for pedestrians
- ☐ **D.** Beware of pedestrians crossing ahead

707 Which is the sign for a ring road?

Mark one answer

☐ **A.** ✗   ☐ **B.**   ☑ **C.** ✓   ☐ **D.**

708 What does this sign mean?

Mark one answer

- ☐ **A.** Route for lorries
- ☑ **B.** Ring road ✓
- ☐ **C.** Rest area
- ☐ **D.** Roundabout

709 What does this sign mean?

Mark one answer

- ☐ **A.** Hilly road
- ☐ **B.** Humps in road
- ☑ **C.** Holiday route ✓
- ☐ **D.** Hospital route

710 What does this sign mean?

Mark one answer

- ☐ **A.** The right-hand lane ahead is narrow
- ☐ **B.** Right-hand lane for buses only
- ☐ **C.** Right-hand lane for turning right
- ☑ **D.** The right-hand lane is closed ✓

711 What does this sign mean?

Mark one answer

- ☐ **A.** Change to the left lane
- ☐ **B.** Leave at the next exit
- ☑ **C.** Contraflow system ✓
- ☐ **D.** One-way street

712 To avoid an accident when entering a contraflow system, you should

Mark three answers
- [x] **A.** Reduce speed in good time ✓
- [ ] **B.** Switch lanes anytime to make progress
- [x] **C.** Choose an appropriate lane early ✓
- [x] **D.** Keep the correct separation distance ✓
- [ ] **E.** Increase speed to pass through quickly
- [ ] **F.** Follow other motorists closely to avoid long queues

713 What does this sign mean?

Mark one answer
- [ ] **A.** Leave motorway at next exit
- [x] **B.** Lane for heavy and slow vehicles ✓
- [ ] **C.** All lorries use the hard shoulder
- [ ] **D.** Rest area for lorries

714 You see this traffic light ahead. Which light(s) will come on next?

Mark one answer
- [x] **A.** Red alone ✓
- [ ] **B.** Red and amber together
- [ ] **C.** Green and amber together
- [ ] **D.** Green alone

715 You are approaching a red traffic light. The signal will change from red to

Mark one answer
- [x] **A.** Red and amber, then green ✓
- [ ] **B.** Green, then amber
- [ ] **C.** Amber, then green
- [ ] **D.** Green and amber, then green

716 A red traffic light means

Mark one answer
- [ ] **A.** You should stop unless turning left
- [ ] **B.** Stop, if you are able to brake safely
- [x] **C.** You must stop and wait behind the stop line ✓
- [ ] **D.** Proceed with caution

717 At traffic lights, amber on its own means

Mark one answer
- [ ] **A.** Prepare to go
- [ ] **B.** Go if the way is clear
- [ ] **C.** Go if no pedestrians are crossing
- [x] **D.** Stop at the stop line ✓

718 A red traffic light means

Mark one answer

- [x] **A.** You must stop behind the white stop line ✓
- [ ] **B.** You may drive straight on if there is no other traffic
- [ ] **C.** You may turn left if it is safe to do so
- [ ] **D.** You must slow down and prepare to stop if traffic has started to cross

719 You are approaching traffic lights. Red and amber are showing. This means

Mark one answer

- [ ] **A.** Pass the lights if the road is clear
- [ ] **B.** There is a fault with the lights – take care
- [x] **C.** Wait for the green light before you pass the lights ✓
- [ ] **D.** The lights are about to change to red

720 You are at a junction controlled by traffic lights. When should you NOT proceed at green?

Mark one answer

- [ ] **A.** When pedestrians are waiting to cross
- [x] **B.** When your exit from the junction is blocked ✓
- [ ] **C.** When you think the lights may be about to change
- [ ] **D.** When you intend to turn right

721 You are in the left-hand lane at traffic lights. You are waiting to turn left. At which of these traffic lights must you NOT move on?

Mark one answer

- [x] **A.**
- [ ] **B.**
- [ ] **C.**
- [ ] **D.**

722 What does this sign mean?

Mark one answer

- [x] **A.** Traffic lights out of order ✓
- [ ] **B.** Amber signal out of order
- [ ] **C.** Temporary traffic lights ahead
- [ ] **D.** New traffic lights ahead

723 You see this sign at a crossroads. You should

Mark one answer

- [ ] **A.** Maintain the same speed
- [x] **B.** Drive on with great care ✓
- [ ] **C.** Find another route
- [ ] **D.** Telephone the police

724 When traffic lights are out of order, who has priority?

Mark one answer

- [ ] **A.** Traffic going straight on
- [ ] **B.** Traffic turning right
- [x] **C.** Nobody ✓
- [ ] **D.** Traffic turning left

725 These flashing red lights mean STOP. In which THREE of the following places could you find them?

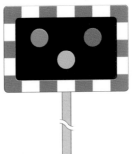

Mark three answers

- [ ] **A.** Pelican crossings
- [x] **B.** Lifting bridges ✓
- [ ] **C.** Zebra crossings
- [x] **D.** Level crossings ✓
- [ ] **E.** Motorway exits
- [x] **F.** Fire stations ✓

726 What do these zigzag lines at pedestrian crossings mean?

Mark one answer

- [x] **A.** No parking at any time ✓
- [ ] **B.** Parking allowed only for a short time
- [ ] **C.** Slow down to 20mph
- [ ] **D.** Sounding horns is not allowed

727 You are approaching a zebra crossing where pedestrians are waiting. Which arm signal might you give?

Mark one answer

- [x] **A.**
- [ ] **B.**

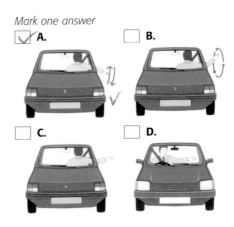

- [ ] **C.**
- [ ] **D.**

728 The white line along the side of the road

Mark one answer

- [x] **A.** Shows the edge of the carriageway ✓
- [ ] **B.** Shows the approach to a hazard
- [ ] **C.** Means no parking
- [ ] **D.** Means no overtaking

729 The white line painted in the centre of the road means

Mark one answer

- [ ] **A.** The area is hazardous and you must not overtake
- [ ] **B.** You should give priority to oncoming vehicles
- [✓] **C.** Do not cross the line unless the road ahead is clear ✓
- [ ] **D.** The area is a national speed limit zone

730 When may you cross a double solid white line in the middle of the road?

Mark one answer

- [ ] **A.** To pass traffic that is queuing back at a junction
- [ ] **B.** To pass a car signalling to turn left ahead
- [✓] **C.** To pass a road maintenance vehicle travelling at 10mph or less
- [ ] **D.** To pass a vehicle that is towing a trailer

731 A white line like this along the centre of the road is a

Mark one answer
- [ ] **A.** Bus lane marking
- [✓] **B.** Hazard warning
- [ ] **C.** 'Give way' marking
- [ ] **D.** Lane marking

732 You see this white arrow on the road ahead. It means

Mark one answer
- [ ] **A.** Entrance on the left
- [ ] **B.** All vehicles turn left
- [✓] **C.** Keep left of the hatched markings ✓
- [ ] **D.** Road bending to the left

733 What does this road marking mean?

Mark one answer
- [ ] **A.** Do not cross the line
- [ ] **B.** No stopping allowed
- [✓] **C.** You are approaching a hazard
- [ ] **D.** No overtaking allowed

734 This marking appears on the road just before a

Mark one answer
- [ ] **A.** No entry sign
- [✓] **B.** Give way sign ✓
- [ ] **C.** Stop sign
- [ ] **D.** No through road sign

Road and traffic signs

735 Where would you see this road marking?

Mark one answer
- **A.** At traffic lights
- **B.** On road humps ✓
- **C.** Near a level crossing
- **D.** At a box junction

736 Which is a hazard warning line?

Mark one answer
- **A.**
- **B.** ✓
- **C.**
- **D.**

737 At this junction there is a stop sign with a solid white line on the road surface. Why is there a stop sign here?

Mark one answer
- **A.** Speed on the major road is de-restricted
- **B.** It is a busy junction
- **C.** Visibility along the major road is restricted ✓
- **D.** There are hazard warning lines in the centre of the road

738 You see this line across the road at the entrance to a roundabout. What does it mean?

Mark one answer
- **A.** Give way to traffic from the right ✓
- **B.** Traffic from the left has right of way
- **C.** You have right of way
- **D.** Stop at the line

739 Where would you find this road marking?

Mark one answer
- **A.** At a railway crossing
- **B.** At a junction ✓
- **C.** On a motorway
- **D.** On a pedestrian crossing

740 How will a police officer in a patrol vehicle normally get you to stop?

Mark one answer
- **A.** Flash the headlights, indicate left and point to the left ✓
- **B.** Wait until you stop, then approach you
- **C.** Use the siren, overtake, cut in front and stop
- **D.** Pull alongside you, use the siren and wave you to stop

741 There is a police car following you. The police officer flashes the headlights and points to the left. What should you do?

Mark one answer
- [ ] **A.** Turn at the next left
- [✓] **B.** Pull up on the left ✓
- [ ] **C.** Stop immediately
- [ ] **D.** Move over to the left

742 You approach a junction. The traffic lights are not working. A police officer gives this signal. You should

Mark one answer
- [ ] **A.** Turn left only
- [ ] **B.** Turn right only
- [ ] **C.** Stop level with the officer's arm
- [✓] **D.** Stop at the stop line ✓

743 The driver of the car in front is giving this arm signal. What does it mean?

Mark one answer
- [ ] **A.** The driver is slowing down
- [ ] **B.** The driver intends to turn right
- [ ] **C.** The driver wishes to overtake
- [✓] **D.** The driver intends to turn left ✓

744 The driver of this car is giving an arm signal. What is he about to do?

Mark one answer
- [ ] **A.** Turn to the right
- [✓] **B.** Turn to the left ✓
- [ ] **C.** Go straight ahead
- [ ] **D.** Let pedestrians cross

745 Which arm signal tells a following vehicle that you intend to turn left?

Mark one answer
- [✓] **A.**
- [ ] **B.**
- [ ] **C.**
- [ ] **D.**

746 How should you give an arm signal to turn left?

Mark one answer
- [ ] **A.**
- [ ] **B.**
- [✓] **C.**
- [ ] **D.**

747 You are signalling to turn right in busy traffic. How would you confirm your intention safely?

Mark one answer
- [ ] **A.** Sound the horn
- [x] **B.** Give an arm signal ✓
- [ ] **C.** Flash your headlamp
- [ ] **D.** Position over the centre line

748 You want to turn right at a junction but you think that your indicators cannot be seen clearly. What should you do?

Mark one answer
- [ ] **A.** Get out and check if your indicators can be seen
- [ ] **B.** Stay in the left-hand lane
- [ ] **C.** Keep well over to the right
- [x] **D.** Give an arm signal as well as an indicator signal ✓

749 When may you sound the horn on your vehicle?

Mark one answer
- [ ] **A.** To give you right of way
- [ ] **B.** To attract a friend's attention
- [x] **C.** To warn others of your presence ✓
- [ ] **D.** To make slower drivers move over

750 You must not use your horn when your vehicle is stationary

Mark one answer
- [x] **A.** Unless a moving vehicle may cause you danger
- [ ] **B.** At any time whatsoever
- [ ] **C.** Unless it is used only briefly
- [ ] **D.** Except for signalling that you have just arrived

751 When motorists flash their headlights at you it means

Mark one answer
- [ ] **A.** That there is a radar speed trap ahead
- [ ] **B.** That they are giving way to you
- [x] **C.** That they are warning you of their presence ✓
- [ ] **D.** That there is something wrong with your vehicle

752 Why should you make sure that you have cancelled your indicators after turning?

Mark one answer
- [ ] **A.** To avoid flattening the battery
- [x] **B.** To avoid misleading other road users ✓
- [ ] **C.** To avoid dazzling other road users
- [ ] **D.** To avoid damage to the indicator relay

753 You are waiting at a T-junction. A vehicle is coming from the right with the left signal flashing. What should you do?

Mark one answer
- [ ] **A.** Move out and accelerate hard
- [x] **B.** Wait until the vehicle starts to turn in
- [ ] **C.** Pull out before the vehicle reaches the junction
- [ ] **D.** Move out slowly

---

754 When may you use hazard warning lights when driving?

Mark one answer
- [ ] **A.** Instead of sounding the horn in a built-up area between 11.30pm and 7am
- [x] **B.** On a motorway or unrestricted dual carriageway, to warn of a hazard ahead
- [ ] **C.** On rural routes, after a warning sign of animals
- [ ] **D.** On the approach to toucan crossings where cyclists are waiting to cross

---

755 Where would you see these road markings?

Mark one answer
- [ ] **A.** At a level crossing
- [x] **B.** On a motorway slip road
- [ ] **C.** At a pedestrian crossing
- [ ] **D.** On a single-track road

---

756 When may you NOT overtake on the left?

Mark one answer
- [x] **A.** On a free-flowing motorway or dual carriageway
- [ ] **B.** When the traffic is moving slowly in queues
- [ ] **C.** On a one-way street
- [ ] **D.** When the car in front is signalling to turn right

---

757 You are driving on a motorway. There is a slow-moving vehicle ahead. On the back you see this sign. You should

Mark one answer
- [ ] **A.** Pass on the right
- [x] **B.** Pass on the left
- [ ] **C.** Leave at the next exit
- [ ] **D.** Drive no further

---

758 What does this motorway sign mean?

Mark one answer
- [x] **A.** Change to the lane on your left
- [ ] **B.** Leave the motorway at the next exit
- [ ] **C.** Change to the opposite carriageway
- [ ] **D.** Pull up on the hard shoulder

759 What does this motorway sign mean?

Mark one answer

- [ ] **A.** Temporary minimum speed 50mph
- [ ] **B.** No services for 50 miles
- [ ] **C.** Obstruction 50 metres (164 feet) ahead
- [x] **D.** Temporary maximum speed 50mph ✓

760 What does this sign mean?

Mark one answer

- [ ] **A.** Through traffic to use left lane
- [ ] **B.** Right-hand lane T-junction only
- [x] **C.** Right-hand lane closed ahead ✓
- [ ] **D.** 11 tonne weight limit

761 On a motorway this sign means

Mark one answer

- [ ] **A.** Move over onto the hard shoulder
- [ ] **B.** Overtaking on the left only
- [ ] **C.** Leave the motorway at the next exit
- [x] **D.** Move to the lane on your left ✓

762 What does '25' mean on this motorway sign?

Mark one answer

- [ ] **A.** The distance to the nearest town
- [ ] **B.** The route number of the road
- [x] **C.** The number of the next junction ✓
- [ ] **D.** The speed limit on the slip road

763 You are driving on a motorway. Red flashing lights appear above your lane only. What should you do?

Mark one answer

- [ ] **A.** Continue in that lane and await further information
- [x] **B.** Go no further in that lane ✓
- [ ] **C.** Drive onto the hard shoulder
- [ ] **D.** Stop and wait for an instruction to proceed

764 The right-hand lane of a three-lane motorway is

Mark one answer

- [ ] **A.** For lorries only
- [x] **B.** An overtaking lane ✓
- [ ] **C.** The right-turn lane
- [ ] **D.** An acceleration lane

765 Where can you find reflective amber studs on a motorway?

Mark one answer
- **A.** Separating the slip road from the motorway
- **B.** On the left-hand edge of the road
- ✓ **C.** On the right-hand edge of the road ✓
- **D.** Separating the lanes

766 Where on a motorway would you find green reflective studs?

Mark one answer
- **A.** Separating driving lanes
- **B.** Between the hard shoulder and the carriageway
- ✓ **C.** At slip road entrances and exits ✓
- **D.** Between the carriageway and the central reservation

767 You are travelling along a motorway. You see this sign. You should

Mark one answer
- ✓ **A.** Leave the motorway at the next exit ✓
- **B.** Turn left immediately
- **C.** Change lane
- **D.** Move onto the hard shoulder

768 You see these signs overhead on the motorway. They mean

Mark one answer
- ✓ **A.** Leave the motorway at the next exit ✓
- **B.** All vehicles use the hard shoulder
- **C.** Sharp bend to the left ahead
- **D.** Stop, all lanes ahead closed

769 What does this sign mean?

Mark one answer
- **A.** No motor vehicles
- ✓ **B.** End of motorway ✓
- **C.** No through road
- **D.** End of bus lane

770 Which of these signs means that the national speed limit applies?

Mark one answer
- **A.**
- **B.**
- **C.**
- ✓ **D.** ✓

771 What is the maximum speed on a single carriageway road?

Mark one answer
- **A.** 50mph
- ✓ **B.** 60mph ✓
- **C.** 40mph
- **D.** 70mph

772 To drive on the road learners MUST

Mark one answer
- **A.** Have no penalty points on their licence
- **B.** Have taken professional instruction
- ☑ **C.** Have a signed, valid provisional licence ✓
- **D.** Apply for a driving test within 12 months

773 To supervise a learner driver you must

Mark two answers
- ☑ **A.** Have held a full licence for at least three years ✓
- ☑ **B.** Be at least 21 ✓
- **C.** Be an approved driving instructor
- **D.** Hold an advanced driving certificate

774 Your driving licence must be signed by

Mark one answer
- **A.** A police officer
- **B.** A driving instructor
- **C.** Your next of kin
- ☑ **D.** Yourself

775 For which TWO of these must you show your motor insurance certificate?

Mark two answers
- **A.** When you are taking your driving test
- **B.** When buying or selling a vehicle
- ☑ **C.** When a police officer asks you for it ✓
- ☑ **D.** When you are taxing your vehicle -
- **E.** When having an MOT inspection -

776 Vehicle excise duty is often called 'Road Tax' or 'The Tax Disc'. You must

Mark one answer
- **A.** Keep it with your registration document
- ☑ **B.** Display it clearly on your vehicle ✓
- **C.** Keep it concealed safely in your vehicle
- **D.** Carry it on you at all times

777 A police officer asks to see your driving documents. You do not have them with you. You may produce them at a police station within   NI

Mark one answer
- **A.** Five days
- ☑ **B.** Seven days ✓
- **C.** 14 days
- **D.** 21 days

778 Before driving anyone else's motor vehicle you should make sure that

Mark one answer
- **A.** The vehicle owner has third party insurance cover
- **B.** Your own vehicle has insurance cover
- ☑ **C.** The vehicle is insured for your use ✓
- **D.** The owner has left the insurance documents in the vehicle

779 What is the legal minimum insurance cover you must have to drive on public roads?

Mark one answer
- **A.** Third party, fire and theft
- **B.** Fully comprehensive
- ☑ **C.** Third party only ✓
- **D.** Personal injury cover

780 Your car has third party insurance. What does this cover?

Mark three answers
- [ ] **A.** Damage to your own car
- [ ] **B.** Damage to your car by fire
- [x] **C.** Injury to another person ✓
- [x] **D.** Damage to someone's property ✓
- [x] **E.** Damage to other vehicles ✓
- [ ] **F.** Injury to yourself

781 The cost of your insurance may be reduced if

Mark one answer
- [ ] **A.** Your car is large and powerful
- [ ] **B.** You are using the car for work purposes
- [ ] **C.** You have penalty points on your licence
- [x] **D.** You are over 25 years old ✓

782 Motor cars and motorcycles must FIRST have an MOT test certificate when they are

Mark one answer NI
- [ ] **A.** One year old
- [x] **B.** Three years old ✓
- [ ] **C.** Five years old
- [ ] **D.** Seven years old

783 An MOT certificate is normally valid for

Mark one answer
- [ ] **A.** Three years after the date it was issued
- [ ] **B.** 10,000 miles
- [x] **C.** One year after the date it was issued ✓
- [ ] **D.** 30,000 miles

784 Your car needs an MOT certificate. If you drive without one this could invalidate your

Mark one answer
- [ ] **A.** Vehicle service record
- [x] **B.** Insurance
- [ ] **C.** Road tax disc
- [ ] **D.** Vehicle registration document

785 When is it legal to drive a car over three years old without an MOT certificate?

Mark one answer NI
- [ ] **A.** Up to seven days after the old certificate has run out
- [ ] **B.** When driving to an MOT centre to arrange an appointment
- [ ] **C.** Just after buying a second-hand car with no MOT
- [x] **D.** When driving to an appointment at an MOT centre ✓

786 Your vehicle needs a current MOT certificate. You do not have one. Until you do have one you will not be able to renew your

Mark one answer
- [ ] **A.** Driving licence
- [ ] **B.** Vehicle insurance
- [x] **C.** Road tax disc ✓
- [ ] **D.** Vehicle registration document

787 Which of these vehicles is NOT required to have an MOT certificate?

Mark two answers

- [ ] **A.** Police vehicle
- [x] **B.** Small trailer
- [ ] **C.** Ambulance
- [x] **D.** Caravan

788 Which THREE of the following do you need before you can drive legally?

Mark three answers

- [x] **A.** A valid signed driving licence
- [x] **B.** A valid tax disc displayed on your vehicle
- [ ] **C.** Proof of your identity
- [x] **D.** Proper insurance cover
- [ ] **E.** Breakdown cover
- [ ] **F.** A vehicle handbook

789 Which THREE pieces of information are found on a vehicle registration document?

Mark three answers

- [x] **A.** Registered keeper
- [x] **B.** Make of the vehicle
- [ ] **C.** Service history details
- [ ] **D.** Date of the MOT
- [ ] **E.** Type of insurance cover
- [x] **F.** Engine size

790 You have a duty to contact the licensing authority when

Mark three answers

- [ ] **A.** You go abroad on holiday
- [x] **B.** You change your vehicle
- [x] **C.** You change your name
- [ ] **D.** Your job status is changed
- [x] **E.** Your permanent address changes
- [ ] **F.** Your job involves travelling abroad

791 You must notify the licensing authority when

Mark three answers

- [x] **A.** Your health affects your driving
- [x] **B.** Your eyesight does not meet a set standard
- [ ] **C.** You intend lending your vehicle
- [ ] **D.** Your vehicle requires an MOT certificate
- [x] **E.** You change your vehicle

792 You have just bought a second-hand vehicle. When should you tell the licensing authority of change of ownership?

Mark one answer

- [x] **A.** Immediately
- [ ] **B.** After 28 days
- [ ] **C.** When an MOT is due
- [ ] **D.** Only when you insure it

793 Which of these items should you carry in your vehicle for use in the event of an accident?

Mark three answers

- [ ] **A.** Road map
- [ ] **B.** Can of petrol
- [ ] **C.** Jump leads
- [x] **D.** Fire extinguisher ✓
- [x] **E.** First Aid kit ✓
- [x] **F.** Warning triangle ✓

794 At the scene of an accident you should

Mark one answer

- [x] **A.** Not put yourself at risk
- [ ] **B.** Go to those casualties who are screaming
- [ ] **C.** Pull everybody out of their vehicles
- [ ] **D.** Leave vehicle engines switched on ✓

795 You are the first to arrive at the scene of an accident. Which FOUR of these should you do?

Mark four answers

- [ ] **A.** Leave as soon as another motorist arrives
- [x] **B.** Switch off the vehicle engine(s) ✓
- [x] **C.** Move uninjured people away from the vehicle(s)
- [x] **D.** Call the emergency services ✓
- [x] **E.** Warn other traffic ✓

796 An accident has just happened. An injured person is lying in the busy road. What is the FIRST thing you should do to help?

Mark one answer

- [ ] **A.** Treat the person for shock
- [x] **B.** Warn other traffic ✓
- [ ] **C.** Place them in the recovery position
- [ ] **D.** Make sure the injured person is kept warm

797 You are the first person to arrive at an accident where people are badly injured. Which THREE should you do?

Mark three answers

- [x] **A.** Switch on your own hazard warning lights ✓
- [x] **B.** Make sure that someone telephones for an ambulance ✓
- [ ] **C.** Try and get people who are injured to drink something
- [ ] **D.** Move the people who are injured clear of their vehicles
- [x] **E.** Get people who are not injured clear of the scene ✓

798 You arrive at the scene of a motorcycle accident. The rider is injured. When should the helmet be removed?

Mark one answer

- [x] **A.** Only when it is essential
- [ ] **B.** Always straight away
- [ ] **C.** Only when the motorcyclist asks
- [ ] **D.** Always, unless they are in shock

799 You arrive at a serious motorcycle accident. The motorcyclist is unconscious and bleeding. Your main priorities should be to

Mark three answers

☑ **A.** Try to stop the bleeding ✓
☐ **B.** Make a list of witnesses
☑ **C.** Check the casualty's breathing ✓
☐ **D.** Take the numbers of the vehicles involved
☐ **E.** Sweep up any loose debris
☑ **F.** Check the casualty's airways ✓

800 You arrive at an accident. A motorcyclist is unconscious. Your FIRST priority is the casualty's

Mark one answer

☑ **A.** Breathing ✓
☐ **B.** Bleeding
☐ **C.** Broken bones
☐ **D.** Bruising

801 At an accident a casualty is unconscious. Which THREE of the following should you check urgently?

Mark three answers

☑ **A.** Circulation
☑ **B.** Airway ✓
☐ **C.** Shock
☑ **D.** Breathing ✓
☐ **E.** Broken bones ✓

802 In First Aid what does ABC stand for?

Mark three answers

☑ **A.** Airway ✓
☐ **B.** Bleeding
☐ **C.** Conscious –
☑ **D.** Breathing ✓
☑ **E.** Circulation
☐ **F.** Alert

803 You arrive at the scene of an accident. It has just happened and someone is unconscious. Which of the following should be given urgent priority to help them?

Mark three answers

☑ **A.** Clear the airway and keep it open ✓
☐ **B.** Try to get them to drink water
☑ **C.** Check that they are breathing ✓
☐ **D.** Look for any witnesses
☑ **E.** Stop any heavy bleeding ✓
☐ **F.** Take the numbers of vehicles involved

804 At an accident someone is unconscious. Your main priorities should be to

Mark three answers

☐ **A.** Sweep up the broken glass
☐ **B.** Take the names of witnesses
☐ **C.** Count the number of vehicles involved
☑ **D.** Check the airway is clear ✓
☑ **E.** Make sure they are breathing ✓
☑ **F.** Stop any heavy bleeding ✓

805 You have stopped at the scene of an accident to give help. Which THREE things should you do?

Mark three answers

- ☑ **A.** Keep injured people warm and comfortable
- ☑ **B.** Keep injured people calm by talking to them reassuringly
- ☐ **C.** Keep injured people on the move by walking them around
- ☐ **D.** Give injured people a warm drink
- ☑ **E.** Make sure that injured people are not left alone

806 You arrive at the scene of an accident. It has just happened and someone is injured. Which of the following should be given urgent priority?

Mark three answers

- ☑ **A.** Stop any severe bleeding
- ☐ **B.** Get them a warm drink
- ☑ **C.** Check that their breathing is OK
- ☐ **D.** Take numbers of vehicles involved
- ☐ **E.** Look for witnesses
- ☑ **F.** Clear their airway and keep it open

807 At an accident a casualty has stopped breathing. You should

Mark two answers

- ☑ **A.** Remove anything that is blocking the mouth
- ☐ **B.** Keep the head tilted forwards as far as possible
- ☐ **C.** Raise the legs to help with circulation
- ☐ **D.** Try to give the casualty something to drink
- ☑ **E.** Keep the head tilted back as far as possible

808 You are at the scene of an accident. Someone is suffering from shock. You should

Mark four answers

- ☑ **A.** Reassure them constantly
- ☐ **B.** Offer them a cigarette
- ☑ **C.** Keep them warm
- ☑ **D.** Avoid moving them if possible
- ☑ **E.** Loosen any tight clothing
- ☐ **F.** give them a warm drink

809 Which of the following should you NOT do at the scene of an accident?

Mark one answer

- ☐ **A.** Warn other traffic by switching on your hazard warning lights
- ☐ **B.** Call the emergency services immediately
- ☑ **C.** Offer someone a cigarette to calm them down
- ☐ **D.** Ask drivers to switch off their engines

810 There has been an accident. The driver is suffering from shock. You should

Mark two answers

- **A.** Give them a drink
- ☑ **B.** Reassure them ✓
- ☑ **C.** Not leave them alone ✓
- **D.** Offer them a cigarette
- **E.** Ask who caused the accident

811 You are at the scene of an accident. Someone is suffering from shock. You should

Mark three answers

- **A.** Offer them a cigarette
- **B.** Offer them a warm drink
- ☑ **C.** Keep them warm ✓
- ☑ **D.** Loosen any tight clothing ✓
- ☑ **E.** Reassure them constantly ✓

812 You have to treat someone for shock at the scene of an accident. You should

Mark one answer

- ☑ **A.** Reassure them constantly ✓
- **B.** Walk them around to calm them down
- **C.** Give them something cold to drink
- **D.** Cool them down as soon as possible

813 You arrive at the scene of a motorcycle accident. No other vehicle is involved. The rider is unconscious, lying in the middle of the road. The first thing you should do is

Mark one answer

- **A.** Move the rider out of the road
- ☑ **B.** Warn other traffic ✓
- **C.** Clear the road of debris
- **D.** Give the rider reassurance

814 At an accident a small child is not breathing. When giving mouth-to-mouth you should blow

Mark one answer

- **A.** Sharply
- ☑ **B.** Gently ✓
- **C.** Heavily
- **D.** Rapidly

815 To start mouth-to-mouth on a casualty you should

Mark three answers

- **A.** Tilt the head forward
- ☑ **B.** Clear the airway ✓
- **C.** Turn them on their side
- ☑ **D.** Tilt their head back ✓
- ☑ **E.** Pinch the nostrils together ✓
- **F.** Put their arms across their chest

816 When you are giving mouth-to-mouth you should only stop when

Mark one answer

- [ ] **A.** You think the casualty is dead
- [✓] **B.** The casualty can breathe without help ✓
- [ ] **C.** The casualty has turned blue
- [ ] **D.** You think the ambulance is coming

817 You arrive at the scene of an accident. There has been an engine fire and someone's hands and arms have been burnt. You should NOT

Mark one answer

- [ ] **A.** Douse the burn thoroughly with cool liquid
- [ ] **B.** Lay the casualty down
- [✓] **C.** Remove anything sticking to the burn ✓
- [ ] **D.** Reassure them constantly

818 You arrive at an accident where someone is suffering from severe burns. You should

Mark one answer

- [ ] **A.** Apply lotions to the injury
- [ ] **B.** Burst any blisters
- [ ] **C.** Remove anything stuck to the burns
- [✓] **D.** Douse the burns with cool liquid ✓

819 You arrive at an accident where someone is suffering from severe burns. You should

Mark one answer

- [ ] **A.** Burst any blisters
- [✓] **B.** Douse the burns thoroughly with cool liquid ✓
- [ ] **C.** Apply lotions to the injury
- [ ] **D.** Remove anything sticking to the burns

820 You arrive at the scene of an accident. A pedestrian has a severe bleeding wound on their leg although it is not broken. What should you do?

Mark two answers

- [ ] **A.** Dab the wound to stop bleeding ✓
- [ ] **B.** Keep both legs flat on the ground
- [✓] **C.** Apply firm pressure to the wound
- [✓] **D.** Raise the leg to lessen bleeding ✓
- [ ] **E.** Fetch them a warm drink

821 You arrive at the scene of an accident. A passenger is bleeding badly from an arm wound. What should you do?

Mark one answer

- [ ] **A.** Apply pressure over the wound and keep the arm down
- [ ] **B.** Dab the wound
- [ ] **C.** Get them a drink
- [✓] **D.** Apply pressure over the wound and raise the arm ✓

822 You arrive at the scene of an accident. A pedestrian is bleeding heavily from a leg wound but the leg is not broken. What should you do?

Mark one answer

- [ ] **A.** Dab the wound to stop the bleeding ✓
- [ ] **B.** Keep both legs flat on the ground
- [✓] **C.** Apply firm pressure to the wound
- [ ] **D.** Fetch them a warm drink

823 At an accident a casualty is unconscious but still breathing. You should only move them if

Mark one answer

- [ ] **A.** An ambulance is on its way
- [ ] **B.** Bystanders advise you to
- [✓] **C.** There is further danger ✓
- [ ] **D.** Bystanders will help you to

824 At an accident you suspect a casualty has back injuries. The area is safe. You should

Mark one answer

- [ ] **A.** Offer them a drink
- [✓] **B.** Not move them ✓
- [ ] **C.** Raise their legs
- [ ] **D.** Offer them a cigarette

825 At an accident it is important to look after the casualty. When the area is safe, you should

Mark one answer

- [ ] **A.** Get them out of the vehicle
- [ ] **B.** Give them a drink
- [ ] **C.** Give them something to eat
- [✓] **D.** Keep them in the vehicle ✓

826 A tanker is involved in an accident. Which sign would show that the tanker is carrying dangerous goods?

Mark one answer

- [ ] **A.** LONG VEHICLE
- [✓] **B.** 2YE 1089 Newtown-on-Moors 0181 645 2830 ✓
- [ ] **C.**
- [ ] **D.**

827 While driving, a warning light on your vehicle's instrument panel comes on. You should

Mark one answer

- **A.** Continue if the engine sounds alright
- **B.** Hope that it is just a temporary electrical fault
- **C.** Deal with the problem when there is more time
- ☑ **D.** Check out the problem quickly and safely ✓

828 For which TWO should you use hazard warning lights?

Mark two answers

- ☑ **A.** When you slow down quickly on a motorway because of a hazard ahead ✓
- ☑ **B.** When you have broken down ✓
- **C.** When you wish to stop on double yellow lines
- **D.** When you need to park on the pavement

829 For which THREE should you use your hazard warning lights?

Mark three answers

- **A.** When you are parking in a restricted area
- ☑ **B.** When you are temporarily obstructing traffic ✓
- ☑ **C.** To warn following traffic of a hazard ahead ✓
- ☑ **D.** When you have broken down ✓
- **E.** When only stopping for a short time

830 When are you allowed to use hazard warning lights?

Mark one answer

- ☑ **A.** When stopped and temporarily obstructing traffic ✓
- **B.** When driving during darkness without headlights
- **C.** When parked for shopping on double yellow lines
- **D.** When travelling slowly because you are lost

831 When should you switch on your hazard warning lights?

Mark one answer

- ☑ **A.** When you cannot avoid causing an obstruction
- **B.** When you are driving slowly due to bad weather
- **C.** When you are towing a broken-down vehicle ✓
- **D.** When you are parked on double yellow lines

832 You have broken down on a two-way road. You have a warning triangle. You should place the warning triangle at least how far from your vehicle?

Mark one answer

- **A.** 5 metres (16 feet)
- **B.** 25 metres (82 feet)
- ☑ **C.** 45 metres (147 feet) ✓
- **D.** 100 metres (328 feet)

833 You are in an accident on a two-way road. You have a warning triangle with you. At what distance before the obstruction should you place the warning triangle?

Mark one answer
- **A.** 25 metres (82 feet)
- ☑ **B.** 45 metres (147 feet) ✓
- **C.** 100 metres (328 feet)
- **D.** 150 metres (492 feet)

834 You have broken down on a two-way road. You have a warning triangle. It should be displayed

Mark one answer
- **A.** On the roof of your vehicle
- **B.** At least 150 metres (492 feet) behind your vehicle
- ☑ **C.** At least 45 metres (147 feet) behind your vehicle ✓
- **D.** Just behind your vehicle

835 The police may ask you to produce which three of these documents following an accident?

Mark three answers
- **A.** Vehicle registration document ✓
- ☑ **B.** Driving licence ✓
- **C.** Theory test certificate
- ☑ **D.** Insurance certificate
- ☑ **E.** MoT test certificate ✓
- **F.** Road tax disc

836 You are involved in an accident with another driver. Someone is injured. Your vehicle is damaged. Which FOUR of the following should you find out?

Mark four answers
- ☑ **A.** Whether the driver owns the other vehicle involved ✓
- ☑ **B.** The other driver's name, address and telephone number ✓
- ☑ **C.** The car make and registration number of the other vehicle ✓
- **D.** The occupation of the other driver
- ☑ **E.** The details of the other driver's vehicle insurance ✓
- **F.** Whether the other driver is licensed to drive

837 You have an accident while driving and someone is injured. You do not produce your insurance certificate at the time. You must report it to the police as soon as possible, or in any case within

NI

Mark one answer
- ☑ **A.** 24 hours ✓
- **B.** 48 hours
- **C.** Five days
- **D.** Seven days

838 At a railway level crossing the red light signal continues to flash after a train has gone by. What should you do?

Mark one answer
- [ ] **A.** Phone the signal operator
- [ ] **B.** Alert drivers behind you
- [x] **C.** Wait ✓
- [ ] **D.** Proceed with caution

839 You break down on a level crossing. The lights have not yet begun to flash. Which THREE things should you do?

Mark three answers
- [x] **A.** Telephone the signal operator ✓
- [x] **B.** Leave your vehicle and get everyone clear ✓
- [ ] **C.** Walk down the track and signal the next train
- [x] **D.** Move the vehicle if a signal operator tells you to ✓
- [ ] **E.** Tell drivers behind what has happened

840 You have stalled in the middle of a level crossing and cannot restart the engine. The warning bell starts to ring. You should

Mark one answer
- [x] **A.** Get out and clear of the crossing ✓
- [ ] **B.** Run down the track to warn the signal operator
- [ ] **C.** Carry on trying to restart the engine
- [ ] **D.** Push the vehicle clear of the crossing

841 Your vehicle has broken down on an automatic railway level crossing. What should you do FIRST?

Mark one answer
- [x] **A.** Get everyone out of the vehicle and clear of the crossing ✓
- [ ] **B.** Phone the signal operator so that trains can be stopped
- [ ] **C.** Walk along the track to give warning to any approaching trains
- [ ] **D.** Try to push the vehicle clear of the crossing as soon as possible

842 Your tyre bursts while you are driving. Which TWO things should you do?

Mark two answers
- [ ] **A.** Pull on the handbrake
- [ ] **B.** Brake as quickly as possible
- [x] **C.** Pull up slowly at the side of the road ✓
- [x] **D.** Hold the steering wheel firmly to keep control ✓
- [ ] **E.** Continue on at a normal speed

843 Which TWO things should you do when a front tyre bursts?

Mark two answers
- [ ] **A.** Apply the handbrake to stop the vehicle
- [ ] **B.** Brake firmly and quickly
- [x] **C.** Let the vehicle roll to a stop ✓
- [ ] **D.** Hold the steering wheel lightly
- [x] **E.** Grip the steering wheel firmly ✓

844 You are driving on the motorway and get a puncture. You should

тряхол колесо?

Mark one answer

- ☑ **A.** Pull onto the hard shoulder as safely as possible
- ☐ **B.** Stop in the lane you are in and change the wheel
- ☐ **C.** Pull into the central reservation as safely as possible ✓
- ☐ **D.** Stop in any lane but use emergency flashers

845 Your vehicle has a puncture on a motorway. What should you do?

Mark one answer

- ☐ **A.** Drive slowly to the next service area to get assistance ✓
- ☐ **B.** Pull up on the hard shoulder. Change the wheel as quickly as possible
- ☑ **C.** Pull up on the hard shoulder. Use the emergency phone to get assistance
- ☐ **D.** Switch on your hazard lights. Stop in your lane

846 You see a car on the hard shoulder of a motorway with a HELP pennant displayed. This means the driver is most likely to be

Mark one answer

- ☑ **A.** A disabled person ✓
- ☐ **B.** First Aid trained
- ☐ **C.** A foreign visitor
- ☐ **D.** A rescue patrol person

847 On the motorway the hard shoulder should be used

Mark one answer

- ☐ **A.** To answer a mobile phone
- ☑ **B.** When an emergency arises ✓
- ☐ **C.** For a short rest when tired
- ☐ **D.** To check a road atlas

848 What TWO safeguards could you take against fire risk to your vehicle?

Mark two answers

- ☐ **A.** Keep water levels above maximum
- ☑ **B.** Carry a fire extinguisher ✓
- ☐ **C.** Avoid driving with a full tank of petrol
- ☐ **D.** Use unleaded petrol ✓
- ☑ **E.** Check out any strong smell of petrol
- ☐ **F.** Use low octane fuel

849 You have broken down on a motorway. When you use the emergency telephone you will be asked

Mark three answers

- ☑ **A.** For the number on the telephone that you are using ✓
- ☐ **B.** For your driving licence details
- ☐ **C.** For the name of your vehicle insurance company ✓
- ☑ **D.** For details of yourself and your vehicle ✓
- ☑ **E.** Whether you belong to a motoring organisation

850 You are on the motorway. Luggage falls from your vehicle. What should you do?

Mark one answer
- ✓ **A.** Stop at the next emergency telephone and contact the police ✓
- **B.** Stop on the motorway and put on hazard lights whilst you pick it up
- **C.** Reverse back up the motorway to pick it up.
- **D.** Pull up on the hard shoulder and wave traffic down

851 You are travelling on a motorway. A suitcase falls from your vehicle. There are valuables in the suitcase. What should you do?

Mark one answer
- **A.** Reverse your vehicle carefully and collect the case as quickly as possible
- **B.** Stop wherever you are and pick up the case but only when there is a safe gap
- ✓ **C.** Stop on the hard shoulder and use the emergency telephone to inform the police ✓
- **D.** Stop on the hard shoulder and then retrieve the suitcase yourself

852 You are driving on a motorway. A large box falls onto the carriageway from a lorry ahead of you. The lorry does not stop. You should

Mark one answer
- ✓ **A.** Drive to the next emergency telephone and inform the police ✓
- **B.** Catch up with the lorry and try to get the driver's attention
- **C.** Stop close to the box and switch on your hazard warning lights until the police arrive
- **D.** Pull over to the hard shoulder, then try and remove the box

853 You are driving on a motorway. When can you use hazard warning lights?

Mark two answers
- **A.** When a vehicle is following too closely
- ✓ **B.** When you slow down quickly because of danger ahead ✓
- **C.** When you are towing another vehicle
- **D.** When driving on the hard shoulder
- ✓ **E.** When you have broken down, on the hard shoulder ✓

854 Overloading your vehicle can seriously affect the

Mark two answers

- [ ] **A.** Gearbox
- [x] **B.** Steering ✓
- [x] **C.** Handling
- [ ] **D.** Battery life
- [ ] **E.** Journey time ✓

855 Who is responsible for making sure that a vehicle is not overloaded?

Mark one answer

- [x] **A.** The driver or rider of the vehicle ✓
- [ ] **B.** The owner of the items being carried
- [ ] **C.** The person who loaded the vehicle
- [ ] **D.** The owner of the vehicle

856 On which TWO occasions might you inflate your tyres to more than the recommended normal pressure?

Mark two answers

- [ ] **A.** When the roads are slippery
- [x] **B.** When driving fast for a long distance ✓
- [ ] **C.** When the tyre tread is worn below 2mm
- [x] **D.** When carrying a heavy load
- [ ] **E.** When the weather is cold
- [ ] **F.** When the vehicle is fitted with anti-lock brakes

857 Any load that is carried on a roof rack MUST be

Mark one answer

- [x] **A.** Securely fastened when driving ✓
- [ ] **B.** Carried only when strictly necessary
- [ ] **C.** As light as possible
- [ ] **D.** Covered with plastic sheeting

858 A heavy load on your roof rack will

Mark one answer

- [ ] **A.** Improve the road holding
- [ ] **B.** Reduce the stopping distance
- [ ] **C.** Make the steering lighter
- [x] **D.** Reduce stability

859 Which THREE are suitable restraints for a child under three years?

Mark three answers

- [x] **A.** A child seat ✓
- [ ] **B.** An adult holding a child
- [ ] **C.** An adult seat belt
- [ ] **D.** A lap belt
- [x] **E.** A harness ✓
- [x] **F.** A baby carrier ✓

860 What do child locks in a vehicle do?

Mark one answer

- [ ] **A.** Lock the seat belt buckles in place
- [ ] **B.** Lock the rear windows in the up position
- [x] **C.** Stop children from opening rear doors ✓
- [ ] **D.** Stop the rear seats from tipping forward

861 Your vehicle is fitted with child safety door locks. You should use these so that children inside the car cannot open

Mark one answer
- [ ] **A.** The right-hand doors
- [ ] **B.** The left-hand doors
- [x] **C.** The rear doors ✓
- [ ] **D.** Any of the doors

862 You should load a trailer so that the weight is

Mark one answer
- [ ] **A.** Mostly over the nearside wheel
- [x] **B.** Evenly distributed ✓
- [ ] **C.** Mainly at the front
- [ ] **D.** Mostly at the rear

863 You are planning to tow a caravan. Which of these will mostly help to aid the vehicle handling?

Mark one answer
- [ ] **A.** A jockey wheel fitted to the towbar
- [ ] **B.** Power steering fitted to the towing vehicle
- [ ] **C.** Anti-lock brakes fitted to the towing vehicle
- [x] **D.** A stabiliser fitted to the towbar

864 Before towing a caravan you should ensure that heavy items in it are loaded

Mark one answer
- [ ] **A.** As high as possible, mainly over the axle(s)
- [x] **B.** As low as possible, mainly over the axle(s) —
- [ ] **C.** As low as possible, forward of the axle(s) —
- [ ] **D.** As high as possible, forward of the axle(s)

865 A trailer must stay securely hitched-up to the towing vehicle. What additional safety device can be fitted to the trailer braking system?

Mark one answer
- [ ] **A.** Stabiliser
- [ ] **B.** Jockey wheel
- [ ] **C.** Corner steadies
- [x] **D.** Breakaway cable

866 If a trailer swerves or snakes when you are towing it you should

Mark one answer
- [x] **A.** Ease off the accelerator and reduce your speed ✓
- [ ] **B.** Let go of the steering wheel and let it correct itself
- [ ] **C.** Brake hard and hold the pedal down
- [ ] **D.** Increase your speed as quickly as possible

867 Are passengers allowed to ride in a caravan that is being towed?

Mark one answer

- [ ] **A.** Yes
- [x] **B.** No ✓
- [ ] **C.** Only if all the seats in the towing vehicle are full
- [ ] **D.** Only if a stabiliser is fitted

868 You are towing a caravan along a motorway. The caravan begins to swerve from side to side. What should you do?

Mark one answer

- [x] **A.** Ease off the accelerator slowly ✓
- [ ] **B.** Steer sharply from side to side
- [ ] **C.** Do an emergency stop
- [ ] **D.** Speed up a little

869 How can you stop a caravan snaking from side to side?

Mark one answer

- [ ] **A.** Turn the steering wheel slowly to each side
- [ ] **B.** Accelerate to increase your speed
- [ ] **C.** Stop as quickly as you can
- [x] **D.** Slow down very gradually ✓

870 You are towing a small trailer on a busy three-lane motorway. All the lanes are open. You must

Mark two answers

- [x] **A.** Not exceed 60mph ✓
- [ ] **B.** Not overtake ✓
- [ ] **C.** Have a stabiliser fitted
- [x] **D.** Use only the left and centre lanes ✓

Alertness

1 C	2 C	3 D	4 AC	5 AB	6 ABCD	7 A	8 B	9 BDF
10 C	11 D	12 ABCD	13 C	14 B	15 D	16 C	17 C	18 C
19 C	20 B	21 D	22 B	23 A	24 C	25 B	26 B	27 B
28 AD	29 A	30 AB	31 C	32 A				

Attitude

33 B	34 D	35 A	36 B	37 A	38 A	39 ACD	40 C	41 A
42 A	43 B	44 C	45 B	46 B	47 A	48 C	49 C	50 D
51 A	52 A	53 D	54 C	55 B	56 D	57 A	58 B	59 C
60 C	61 B	62 B	63 C	64 D	65 B	66 BCD	67 ABE	68 A
69 A	70 D	71 B	72 A	73 A	74 B	75 C	76 B	77 C
78 D	79 A	80 C	81 A	82 C	83 DE	84 B	85 D	86 A

Safety and your vehicle

87 A	88 B	89 BCDF	90 CDE	91 D	92 AB	93 D	94 A	95 D
96 B	97 BC	98 C	99 B	100 B	101 BC	102 B	103 B	104 A
105 D	106 D	107 C	108 C	109 A	110 A	111 A	112 D	113 A
114 B	115 B	116 D	117 ABF	118 ABC	119 B	120 ADE	121 BDF	122 ABF
123 BCD	124 D	125 B	126 A	127 C	128 B	129 C	130 D	131 BEF
132 D	133 AB	134 BDF	135 A	136 AB	137 D	138 D	139 C	140 D
141 A	142 D	143 D	144 CD	145 B	146 B	147 D	148 D	149 ACF
150 C	151 B	152 ABC	153 A	154 D	155 A	156 D	157 B	158 B
159 AE	160 C	161 C						

Safety margins

162 B	163 B	164 D	165 C	166 BC	167 B	168 C	169 B	170 BC
171 C	172 C	173 C	174 B	175 B	176 B	177 A	178 B	179 D
180 B	181 C	182 ACE	183 A	184 A	185 A	186 C	187 B	188 A
189 D	190 D	191 D	192 D	193 D	194 D	195 A	196 B	197 C
198 AE	199 C	200 B	201 D	202 C	203 BDEF	204 B	205 D	206 B
207 D	208 A	209 D	210 C	211 BC	212 B	213 D	214 B	215 C
216 B	217 A	218 AD	219 C	220 A	221 B	222 ACE		

Hazard awareness

223 D	224 CD	225 B	226 C	227 A	228 D	229 B	230 ACE	231 D
232 A	233 C	234 BF	235 B	236 A	237 D	238 C	239 A	240 C

241 B	242 C	243 C	244 C	245 D	246 A	247 C	248 B	249 B
250 CD	251 B	252 D	253 B	254 A	255 AE	256 B	257 A	258 C
259 D	260 A	261 D	262 A	263 ABC	264 B	265 AE	266 C	267 B
268 A	269 D	270 BC	271 C	272 A	273 D	274 D	275 A	276 B
277 D	278 ABD	279 ABC	280 ACE	281 B	282 ABE	283 D	284 AD	285 B
286 C	287 C	288 CD	289 C	290 D	291 C	292 CD	293 AB	294 C
295 B	296 AC	297 AB	298 A	299 A	300 B	301 A	302 B	303 A
304 B	305 ABC	306 A	307 CD	308 ABE	309 BCE	310 A	311 A	312 A
313 A	314 C	315 C						

Vulnerable road users

316 C	317 D	318 C	319 D	320 D	321 C	322 C	323 B	324 B
325 B	326 D	327 C	328 D	329 C	330 B	331 ABE	332 ADE	333 C
334 AE	335 D	336 D	337 AD	338 D	339 D	340 C	341 B	342 C
343 A	344 D	345 C	346 B	347 C	348 A	349 A	350 D	351 D
352 D	353 D	354 B	355 D	356 C	357 B	358 A	359 C	360 D
361 C	362 D	363 C	364 AC	365 B	366 B	367 C	368 C	369 B
370 A	371 B	372 B	373 D	374 C	375 C	376 D	377 D	378 ABC
379 A	380 C	381 C	382 ACE	383 D	384 A	385 B	386 B	387 B
388 D	389 B	390 A	391 A	392 AC	393 D	394 ABD	395 B	396 C
397 B	398 D	399 D	400 A	401 D	402 C	403 B	404 A	

Other types of vehicle

405 B	406 B	407 B	408 A	409 A	410 C	411 B	412 B	413 D
414 D	415 B	416 B	417 B	418 D	419 B	420 B	421 A	422 CD
423 B	424 BC	425 AC	426 B	427 D	428 C	429 A	430 B	431 BD
432 A								

Vehicle handling

433 BD	434 D	435 D	436 BD	437 D	438 C	439 C	440 ACE	441 B
442 ABD	443 A	444 D	445 C	446 D	447 C	448 C	449 B	450 CE
451 C	452 A	453 B	454 D	455 C	456 A	457 B	458 A	459 B
460 A	461 D	462 D	463 C	464 D	465 A	466 B	467 C	468 BD
469 AB	470 A	471 D	472 A	473 ACD	474 B	475 D	476 B	477 D
478 A	479 C	480 C	481 B	482 B	483 D	484 D	485 CD	486 D
487 B	488 A	489 A	490 D	491 DE	492 BE	493 C	494 D	495 ABDF
496 A								